PARENTING IN A TRANSGENDER WORLD

By Erin Brewer, PhD

PARENTING IN A TRANSGENDER WORLD
Erin Brewer, PhD

Cover by Maria Keffler

Copyright © 2022, Advocates Protecting Children
ISBN: 979-8842461394

Advocates Protecting Children
PO Box 41981
Arlington VA, 22204

https://www.advocatesprotectingchildren.org

Email: advocatesprotectingchildren@gmail.com

TABLE OF CONTENTS

Erin Brewer

ACKNOWLEDGMENTS

I am deeply grateful to all those who have spoken out against the transgender ideology that is systematically erasing women's and girls' rights and protections, and encouraging children to believe they were born in the wrong body. If there ever was a time to speak out, it is now.

DEDICATION

To Maria, Anna, Sheri, my Sisters, and for all those who have been harmed by the transgender ideology.

FOREWORD

When I first met Erin Brewer, I had already desisted several months before then. I, like many other young women, had been sucked into the belief that the traits that differentiated me from most other women made me a man. I thought the athleticism, straightforward thinking, and preference for cargo shorts over skirts that drew me to hanging out with boys meant that I actually was one. Thankfully my parents knew otherwise: if they hadn't, I would likely have had my breasts sliced off, my genitals mutilated beyond repair, and my hormonal makeup permanently scarred by puberty blockers and testosterone. Erin, too, adopted a transgender identity as a child; having such similar experiences has drawn us into becoming close friends.

Erin has written many books on the logical corn maze that is transgender ideology; books explaining what's happening in schools, about her experience as a transgender-identified child, and more. *Parenting in a Transgender World* is her compass meant to guide parents through the maze, utilizing the same critical thinking skills that my parents used to navigate this seemingly unescapable labyrinth.

Common sense tells us that femininity and masculinity are only generalizations. I am just as object-focused as most boys, gossip flies over my head like a baseball, and I have suits and short hair instead of dresses and flowing locks. I am extremely athletic, sparring and competing with girls and boys alike. But these things do not indicate *maleness*—they are only hobbies and activities typical for men to prefer. Transgender ideology claims it wipes out sex stereotypes when it only reverses them: it used to be that boys played with trucks, and girls played tea party, and anyone who didn't fit had something inherently wrong with them. Now, anyone who plays with trucks is a boy, and anyone who plays tea party is a girl, and anyone who doesn't fit must be castrated, injected with dangerous chemicals, and dressed up to appear as a caricature of the opposite sex. Any parent who wants to protect their child from being mutilated or from accepting the mutilation of others needs to read this, and all of the other books Erin Brewer has carefully put together for the benefit of mothers and fathers.

I am unfathomably grateful to have met Erin and to have been able to share my story with her. Hopefully this book will allow you to meet a piece of her too—not only her experiences as a transgender-identified child, but her dedication to all children who suffer the same way as she once did. More and more stories like ours are bubbling to the surface, but armed with the knowledge in this book, you can help prevent children from ever walking down that path in the first place.

~ Petra Harangir

INTRODUCTION

"If liberty means anything at all, it means the right to tell people what they do not want to hear."

~ George Orwell[1]

The inspiration for this book came one morning when I was out on a walk with my dear friend and co-founder of Advocates Protecting Children, Maria Keffler. We were musing about all the requests we were getting from parents who wanted to know what they could do to prevent their children from adopting a transgender identity.

One of us said something about how we are living in a transgender world; it is no longer **if** a child will be introduced to transgender ideology, but when. In most cases, it is between preschool and second grade. Parents write to us and tell us they feel like they are on a sinking ship, and transgender ideology is the ocean sucking their children under. Confused and desperate, they know if children get pulled in too deeply, they might drown.

Moms and dads are terrified as they hear about neighbors losing custody of their kids for not accepting that their child was born in the wrong body. Parents feel powerless as children come home from school reporting on classmates assuming the identity of the opposite sex and teachers compelling their children to accept the lie. Mothers and fathers are aghast as they watch teachers on YouTube bragging about undermining parents by encouraging children to adopt a transgender identity while at school, and hide it from their parents. There is increasing apprehension as parents helplessly watch policies being enacted that indoctrinate their children into transgender ideology at the federal, state, and local levels.

Maria and I thought about putting together a brochure to help parents understand both what they are up against, and how they can equip themselves and their families to fight back, but as I started to work on it, I realized it was going to be more than just a brochure.

Explaining the transgender ideology alone is complicated. It is a convoluted belief system held by those indoctrinated into a cult which is based on mystical ideas and contradictory thoughts who advocate for a world in which feelings are more important than facts.

This guide is to help you get up to speed with the transgender ideology and provide you with some ideas for protecting your family.

Unfortunately, there are no guarantees that your child will not be indoctrinated. Even the most proactive families sometimes lose a child to the ideology. For those parents, Maria has written *Desist, Detrans, & Detox: Getting Your Child Out of the Gender Cult.*

Parenting in a Transgender World specifically addresses parents, but it can be used by anyone who is trying to understand transgender ideology and to arm children with skills to resist it.

Sometimes Maria and I feel like we spend all of our time lending a hand to parents who have lost their child to the transgender activists, trying to provide some comfort and resources and encouragement. Unlike someone who drowns in real life, children who have been indoctrinated into the transgender ideology are not completely lost.

With love and patience—and a little luck—these children will recognize how much their parents love them and miss them, and they will realize that creating a fake identity was not authentic and brave, but a rejection of themselves and their family.

When parents contact us saying their child has adopted a transgender identity and want to know how to get their child back, we suggest three things.

- Take the child out of school immediately and either homeschool or find a school that has not caved to the transgender ideology. Schools used to teach children about important skills like critical thinking, math, and writing, but increasingly they are simply recruitment centers for transgender activists.

- Protect the child from peers who have already been indoctrinated into the ideology.
- Take away the child's access to computers and phones, and specifically, social media. If the child needs to have access to computers for schoolwork, supervise the child the entire time he or she is using the computer.

Parents often feel like these steps are too radical or difficult, but parents who have employed these measures consistently report saving their child from the transgender ideology. Some parents don't have the means to pull their child out of school, so it is more challenging for them to help guide their child away from the transgender ideology. It is like trying to help a child with a drug addiction when he or she is hanging out with the dealers every day. It can be done, but it is much more difficult.

It is far better to prevent the drug addiction or the indoctrination into transgender ideology.

Parents often are uncomfortable talking about transgender ideology with children. It is difficult. We want children to maintain their innocence. Talking about transgender ideology often means explaining to children that there are some people who are so confused that they think girls can become boys and boys can become girls. There are people who say ridiculous things like "girls can have penises."

It is hard admitting to ourselves and to our children that society has gone off the rails so profoundly that something as basic as biology is up for debate. It is critical that you introduce children to what is true before others have a chance to peddle falsehoods.

There is something called the *primacy principle*. We have long known that beliefs that are developed in early childhood are hard to dislodge. If children learn about transgender ideology at school or from peers or on social media, it will be much harder for you to deprogram them if you haven't early-on introduced them to biological facts.

The goal of this book is to prevent your children from being recruited into transgender ideology, to stave off the heartbreak of seeing children reject family and friends, as well the very essence of who they are. I wrote this to give you some ideas about how you can provide your child with the skills needed to have a strong sense of self, a solid connection to family, and the ability to reject the ever-increasing attempts at indoctrination.

PART 1: UNDERSTANDING THE TRANSGENDER WORLD

"The great enemy of clear language is insincerity. When there is a gap between one's real and one's declared aims, one turns, as it were, instinctively to long words and exhausted idioms, like a cuttlefish squirting out ink."

~ George Orwell[2]

It is hard to explain just how completely the transgender ideology has captured our world. A decade or two ago, there were a few people who suffered from a severe discomfort with the sex they were born and who identified themselves as transexuals. In the 2000s, transgender activists hitched their wagon to the LGB movement and have systematically undermined the very rights for which the LGB movement was fighting, while also undermining the rights of girls and women while actively grooming vulnerable children into their dangerous belief system.

To illustrate how insidious the transgender ideology is, this is the definition of *gender* from a Family Life education handbook from 2014:

> Gender refers to the socially constructed roles, behaviours, activities and attributes that are considered appropriate for males and females. Most of our ideas about gender are influenced by the messages we get from family, friends, the media, and peers. Both boys and girls tend to feel pressure to behave in a certain way because of these messages. Sometimes gender norms limit opportunities, especially for girls and women. This is called *gender discrimination*.

> Belief in gender equality does not mean that we no longer recognise differences between men and women. It means respecting both sexes and acknowledging that an individual's biological sex should not determine how we see that person's talents, abilities, or general responsibilities. Gender is learnt and therefore can be unlearnt. Attitudes about gender vary from person to person and place to place. They also change over time.[3]

The previous definition makes it clear that gender is a set of learned behaviors that correspond to a given sex.

The term *gender* morphed into *gender identity* as transgender activists confused sex and gender, first saying that gender is performative, then saying it is innate, and then saying that gender and sex are interchangeable and biological.

The successful capturing of language by transgender activists can be seen in the following definition from a comprehensive sexuality education handbook published in 2017:

> Gender identity is the gender that a person feels themselves to be, regardless of their body. Most of the time, a person's biological sex and their gender identify are the same. In other words, a person with a female body feels and identifies herself as a woman. However, some people feel that they are in the wrong body. They are transgender. Some say that they have a female brain trapped in a male body, or the other way around. Some identify with neither genders, some identify with both genders, while others feel they cannot relate to the idea of gender at all. Some transgendered people change their sex by taking hormones and having surgery.[4]

Transgender activists claim to be marginalized while actively oppressing anyone who disagrees with their foundational claim that it is possible to be born in the wrong body. It is important to have a solid understanding of the language and tactics of transgender activists in order to protect your children from those who seek to recruit your children.

Part 1 covers the language being used by transgender activists, the claims they make, the harms of their ideology, and the tactics they use for recruitment.

LANGUAGE

"But if thought corrupts language, language can also corrupt thought. A bad usage can spread by tradition and imitation, even among people who should and do know better."

~ George Orwell[5]

Before figuring out how to parent kids in a world that has been taken over by an ideology which closely resembles a cult, it is important to become familiar with transgender jargon.

The transgender movement has done a remarkable job of taking over words to disguise, distort, and reverse their meaning. In addition, transgender activists have also created nonsensical words that have rapidly been infused into our culture, making it incredibly confusing for those who are not familiar with the ideology.

As a parent, it is important that you know the language and understand how it is designed to confuse children, undermine truth, and identify allies and enemies of the transgender ideology.

Knowing the language of trans will also help you to be on the lookout for signs your child is being indoctrinated. For example, if your child starts referring to mothers as a *birthing people* or calls you *cis*, or says you are transphobic for using someone's *deadname*, then it might be time to get Maria Keffler's book, *Desist, Detrans & Detox—Getting Your Child Out of the Gender Cult.*

THE TRANS UMBRELLA

The *transgender umbrella* is meant to capture anyone who decides to identify as anything other than regressive stereotypes based on sex. In other words, nearly everyone.

According to the National Academic Advising Association's *Trans Umbrella Resource Sheet*, the term *transgender umbrella* describes "someone whose self-identification, anatomy, appearance, manner, expression, behavior, and/or other's perceptions of, challenges traditional societal expectations of congruent gender expression and designated birth sex."[6]

Anyone who doesn't adhere to regressive sex-based stereotypes in thoughts, words, or actions is considered transgender. Or at least I think that is what it means. It is often difficult to pin down words from the transgender ideology because the words are based on feelings where everyone's feelings are valid...as long as they identify as transgender.

As is clear from the Masterlist of Genders,[7] anyone can adopt any kind of identity, no matter how obscure or absurd, and claim their place under the transgender umbrella.

Though this looks farcical, it is not a joke. These are just a few of the genders from the Masterlist of Genders (for a full list, see Endnotes).

Anesigender: feeling like a certain gender, yet being more comfortable identifying with another

Molligender: a gender that is soft, subtle, and subdued

Vapogender: a gender that sort of feels like smoke; can be seen on a shallow level, but once you go deeper, it disappears and you are left with no gender and only tiny wisps of what you thought it was.

Recently I saw a video about *cake gender*, which is someone who identifies as "feeling light and fluffy or sweet and warm."[8]

I suppose someone who identifies as brownie gender is dense and gooey, although perhaps dry and crunchy, depending on how long the gender has been baking in the oven.

The Human Rights Campaign states that *gender identity* is "One's innermost concept of self as male, female, a blend of both or neither—how individuals perceive themselves and what they call themselves."[9]

Conceivably, there can be as many genders as there are people, since it is unlikely that any two people would have exactly the same experience of being male, female, both, neither, or somewhere in between. Even if we did, there would be no way to know for sure, since gender identity is based solely and completely on one's internal sense of self.

If this were just something teens were talking about in high school, it would be similar to previous teen trends. When I was in high school, a number of kids dressed up in wacky outfits and went to *Rocky Horror Picture Show* every Friday night. Another group settled in for the weekend to play Dungeons and Dragons. These kids were pushing social boundaries and typical teen fashion. However, the transgender ideology is far from a normal teen fad. The New York Commission on Human Rights recognizes at least 31 distinct genders that are protected under antidiscrimination law.[10] And Facebook offers 50 different genders users can choose from.[11] Increasingly, laws are being passed that require acceptance and affirmation of an individual's gender identity.

Respecting classmates' gender is increasingly showing up in school policies. Children are being coerced into accepting that a boy can become a girl, a girl can become a boy, and that either can become neither, or both.

Cis

Transgender activists have done a great job of using "transgender" to cover so many different behaviors and identities that nearly everyone has a place under their umbrella. Except for those who have been designated as *cis*.

Cis-gender is a derogatory term used for anyone who does not claim one of the myriad of transgender identities and, according to the activists, "is comfortable with the sex assigned at birth."

One transgender youth group has a weekly meeting called "Cisn't," a so-called inclusive group for everyone but those who don't claim a trans identity. Groups like this make it uncool not to identify as trans.[12]

The only ones who are not included are what the activists call *cis-gender*. Anyone who rejects transgender ideology, including gays and lesbians who don't accept transgender ideology, are ostracized.

Using the term *cis* allows the activists to control language in a way that undermines reality. By using or accepting the use of the term, one is accepting one of the basic foundational beliefs of the trans ideology—that our sex is based on feelings and external appearance or behavior, rather than being a biological reality.

No wonder so many people take cover under the trans umbrella. I don't know a single person who is 100% comfortable with being male or female. Imagine how confusing it must be for children who are told that their gender is based on an internal sense of self, which is based on stereotypes of what it means to be male or female. No wonder so many children are adopting a trans identity!

These kids are also deceived into believing that any discomfort they have is because they are not cis-gender, when nearly everyone struggles at some point in their life with discomfort about their body or fitting in with their peers.

Self-Identification (Self-ID)

Self-ID suggests that all we should have to do is declare our gender identity for it to be a legally accepted fact. If a man says he is a woman, he is a woman. If a woman says she is a man, she is a man. If a child says she is gender fluid—moving back and forth between being a boy and a girl—she is both male and female. In other words, self-ID means that a man who says he is a woman isn't a man pretending to be a woman, or a man who feels like he is a woman. He somehow becomes a woman. Legally.

As one man who says he is a woman stated in a legislative hearing in Idaho, "My name is Emily Jackson Edney, and my pronouns are she, her, and hers. I don't identify as a woman. I am a woman."[13]

Because of laws that have been enacted both nationally and internationally, a man like Emily is able to change his birth certificate, drivers' license, and passport to list him as female, giving him the right to access any space reserved for women. Self-ID allows people to retroactively change their sex at birth based solely on their desire to be recognized as the opposite sex. A man isn't required to have his penis removed or shave his beard; he just has to file paperwork to get his birth certificate altered. Self-ID is not the law of the land everywhere but it is increasingly being accepted. In fact, in some states, even children can have birth certificates altered if their parents accept that the child was born in the wrong body.[14]

Most people assume that in order for a transgender-identified male to get his birth certificate changed, he has to undergo what is euphemistically called a *sex change operation*: having his genitals removed and undergoing hormonal treatments to feminize his body. In her book *Trans: When Ideology Meets Reality*,[15] Helen Joyce does an excellent job of tracing how self-ID laws have stealthily been passed without the general population having a clue that these laws allow any man to legally become a woman. The result has been devastating, as rapists in male prisons recognize that they can simply claim to be a woman and insist upon being relocated to women-only prisons. Sex offenders no longer have to contrive ways to spy on unsuspecting women in bathrooms and showers, they simply declare themselves to be women, gaining legal access to spaces where women undress and attend to intimate personal hygiene.

Trans widows, wives who have lost their husbands after they self-ID as a woman, are often encouraged by therapists to embrace the husband's new identity as lesbian in what can only be considered *coercive conversion therapy*. Men can not only become women but they can turn their wives into lesbians with self-ID.

Actual lesbians (females attracted to females), on the other hand, are coerced into accepting men with penises as lovers. Lesbians who do not accept men who self-ID as women as sexual partners are accused of being hateful and cruel for having "genital preferences."[16]

Transphobic

This is a catchall word that is thrown at anyone who does not agree 100% with the dictates of the transgender ideology. For example, anyone who believes that biological males should not pretend to be women and compete in women's sports. Transphobic. Anyone who is concerned about physically intact men claiming to be women and insisting they have a right to use women's bathrooms, locker rooms, and showers. Transphobic. Anyone who is concerned that children are being told that they are inherently flawed and should kill who they are and create a fake persona. Transphobic. Anyone who thinks it isn't safe to allow men who have been convicted of violent sexual crimes to be housed in women's prisons. Transphobic.

Because *transphobia* is considered hateful, anyone accused of being transphobic is viewed as not just the enemy, but less than human, and therefore not worthy or deserving of basic human rights and protections.

Preferred Pronouns

Transgender activists talk about their "preferred" pronouns, but to be clear, these pronouns are not preferred—they are coerced and compelled. Men can insist on being referred to as "she" in the workplace and file sexual harassment charges if co-workers fail to use "she/her/hers" pronouns.

Increasingly, children are being disciplined at school for not using a classmate's chosen pronouns.[17]

Teachers are fired for not calling a female student "he."[18]

As confusing as this is, it gets worse. Not only can a man insist on being called "she," anyone can insist that others use any number of neopronouns, from "ze/zem/zir" to "fe/fay/fur."

15

Anyone can make up any gender identity and accompanying pronouns. Those who identify as *gender fluid* can have changing pronouns as they flow from one gender to another.

Imagine a teacher having to focus on getting student's pronouns right during lessons, knowing a slipup can result in termination. The teacher will be so focused on not offending his students, he will hardly be able to teach. Or a doctor treating what is clearly a female body, but she has to refer to her patient using male pronouns, as well as use the names for body parts her patient wants, such as *shenis* for a clitoris.

Misgendering

Preferred pronouns lead us right into misgendering.

Misgendering is the offense of using what someone decides are the wrong pronouns. As a result of self-ID, individuals don't have to change anything about their appearance to identify as the opposite sex, or both sexes, or neither sex, or a completely fantastical made-up sex. They also get to dictate what pronouns others use.

In some states, parents who insist on using the correct pronouns rather than a child's preferred pronouns are charged with abuse. Policy allows people to force others to use made-up pronouns or incorrect pronouns, or face serious repercussions for misgendering.

Deadname

Another way in which transgender activists can compel speech is by making up new names for themselves. This is different from a nickname that people can choose to use or not. This is a new name, and the name given at birth is considered a *deadname*. To use a deadname is considered crass, at the very least. Many in the transgender community consider it physical violence, minimizing the pain and trauma of people who have experienced actual abuse.

The term itself provides important insights into the transgender ideology. It suggests that someone who assumes a new gender identity isn't going through the normal process of changing that all people do as they mature and learn and have new experiences. This isn't like someone converting from Catholicism to Judaism, or a Republican becoming a Democrat, or a vegan deciding to eat meat. Instead it is someone who has metaphysically killed who they are in an attempt to become someone new. The deadname is a reminder of the person who they are trying to replace with a new persona.

Chest-Feeding Birthing Parent

Pronouns and deadnames are not the only instances of compelled speech. Under the auspice of inclusion—the idea that we wouldn't want to make anyone feel left out or marginalized—trans activists have systematically rewritten our language. Women who have children are no longer *mothers*, they are *birthing people*. Mothers who nurse their babies are called *chest feeders*. Sisters and brothers are *siblings* and nieces and nephews are *niblings*. Women who are reduced to nothing more than bodily functions: A woman is no longer a dignified human being—she is a *front hole*, a *cervix-haver*, a *menstrator*. At the same time, only men who say they are women are considered real women.

This manipulation of language has taken over society. In early 2021, the US Congress changed its rules to exclude sex-specific roles such as *mother*, *father*, *son*, *daughter*, *brother*, and *sister*. In addition, no person would be referred to as *he* or *him* or *she* or *her*. All individuals are now referred to as *they*.

Ironically, the term *mother*, according to transgender activists, should be replaced with *birthing person*. However, fathers who decide they are women are encouraged to call themselves *mother*, leading back to the notion that men who say they are women are more authentically women than actual adult human females.

Affirmation

Though the idea of affirmation sounds great, transgender activists have completely turned the idea upside down. Affirmation usually means supporting someone by validating who they are. In transgender jargon, *affirmation* means encouraging someone to disassociate from who they are and embrace a fake persona. In addition, *affirmation* now means "celebrating medical interventions that damage an otherwise healthy body in order to feminize, masculinize, or neuter the person to match a self-proclaimed gender-identity." Affirmation is the linchpin of the entire ideology. It insists society accept the transgender ideology under the guise of affirmation. It dictates that one listens to those claiming a transgender identity's every demand without question, no matter the emotional, physical, or practical cost.

Parents are often told that failure to affirm their child's newfound identity will result in their child's death by suicide.

Affirmative Care

Transgender activists insist that children who adopt a transgender identity have access to what they inaccurately claim to be "lifesaving care" and "medically necessary care."

What they are calling for are experimental interventions that damage an otherwise-healthy child's body and have lifelong side effects and complications. I have included a short chapter about the known harms of puberty blockers and cross-sex hormones; however, it should be clear that no child should ever be given the message that altering his or her appearance simply for cosmetic reasons is medically necessary.

Safe

Anyone who believes the transgender ideology is considered *safe*. Anyone who doesn't is considered *unsafe*. Teachers often refer to parents who do not accept transgender ideology as unsafe, thus undermining children's relationships with parents and other adults. This is incredibly damaging, as it confuses children about who really is safe. For example, a mother who doesn't affirm the transgender identity of her daughter is considered unsafe, but adults within the transgender community are considered safe, even if they are predatory, simply because they affirm the child's gender identity.

Surgery: Top and Bottom

Part of the affirmative-care model for children is elective cosmetic surgery. The language is obscured so people don't grasp what is actually happening to children.

Girls as young as 13 have radical mastectomies. Both breasts removed, and often the nipples are removed, leaving grotesque scaring across the chest and muscle damage that will never fully heal. This surgery is called *top surgery*.

Transgender activists will often deny that young teen girls have this surgery, but there is documentation of it nonetheless. In a video with Johanna Olson-Kennedy, director of the LA Children's Hospital gender clinic, she dismissed concerns that radical cosmetic surgery might lead to regrets later in life. "If you want breasts at a later point in your life, you can go and get them." During this video she also shared documentation of 13–17-year-old girls whose breasts were removed as part of a research project.[19]

It is not uncommon for girls as young as 15 to be approved for a double mastectomy by insurance companies that have capitulated to the ideology.[20]

Bottom surgery is any elective cosmetic surgery involving the genitals. Transgender activist Kellyn Lakhardt, of the Kaiser Permanente, admits unashamedly that a 16-year-old boy had a vaginoplasty.

Vaginoplasty is incredibly invasive surgery, with poor outcomes and long-term complications. In addition, it results in permanent sterilization. It involves removal of the testicles, removal of the penis, and the creation of a wound between the teen's legs to serve as a fake vagina.

Top and bottom surgeries are elective cosmetic and irreparable, resulting in lifelong dysfunction. They have not been shown to be an effective treatment for gender dysphoria.

Hate Speech

This is simple.

Using any language transgender activists dislike under any circumstances is considered hate speech.

TERF

This is an interesting term.

The letters stand for *transgender-exclusionary radical feminist*. The term came about to describe women who did not accept the self-ID of men who claimed to be women. Radical feminism is based on the belief that patriarchy needs to be destroyed.

The term TERF now is applied to anyone who doesn't affirm the transgender ideology, and is therefore transphobic and guilty of hate speech. It is odd to see conservative Christian men accused of being TERFs since they are not, by any stretch of the imagination, radical feminists.

Suicide

It might seem strange to define suicide. Most people understand what it means; however, transgender activists are using suicide in what can only described as a despicable and deceptively manipulative way. They claim that children will kill themselves if parents use their given name and the correct pronouns. If kids are not allowed to use the bathroom, locker room, and shower of the opposite sex. If they're not allowed to compete in sports of the opposite sex. If kids are not allowed access to puberty blockers, cross-sex hormones, and surgery. And in what is the most blatant emotional blackmail of all, they claim that any efforts to change policy or law in a way that they don't want will result in children killing themselves. They say that anyone who disagrees with them in any way has blood on their hands.

Parents are coerced into affirming their child because they are admonished, "You can have a dead daughter or a live son," or "You can have a live daughter or a dead son."

So-called affirmation is marketed as *suicide prevention*.

The innumerable harms of puberty blockers, cross-sex hormones, and cosmetic surgeries are brushed under the rug. Activists claim transing children is "lifesaving medical treatment," because if trans-identified–children don't get everything they demand, they will kill themselves.

Since when is giving children everything they want when they want it an acceptable or healthy parenting strategy?

Common sense says that giving a child everything he or she wants without reserve will create an emotionally unstable and manipulative child. But this is exactly what transgender activists are vying for.

Threats of suicide are not only emotional blackmail, they are also dangerous. Such rhetoric communicates to children that they are unable to navigate difficult feelings, and if they don't get what they want, the appropriate response is suicide.

Transgender activists train children to manipulate others to get what they want.

Canadian psychologist Dr. Wallace Wong, who makes a living by encouraging kids to transition, was recorded during a video presentation to parents and children at a public library. He told the audience, "Pull a stunt. Suicide every time. They will give you what you need."[21]

In other words, fake a suicide attempt in order to manipulate others to give vulnerable children what they have been convinced they need by transgender activists.

Detransitioners have reported being coached to threaten suicide, and even to stage a suicide attempt, in order to get what they want.

Some populations have historically suffered horrific oppression: slavery, concentration camps, genocide. They were not forced to kill themselves, instead they persevered incredibly difficult situations. How is calling someone by a pronoun he or she doesn't like justification for suicide?

In addition, suicide is a known social contagion. In other words, telling children they will kill themselves is likely to result in children killing themselves.

The American Foundation for Suicide Research cautions reporters that when reporting on suicide, they should not report that "a suicide death was 'caused' by a single event ... since research shows no one takes their life for one single reason, but rather a combination of factors."[22] Unfortunately, advocacy groups and irresponsible media are tempted to use the tragedy of a those taking their own life for political purposes.

The Senior Clinical Neuropsychologist for the State of Texas, Dr. Alan Hopewell, testified in early 2021 that he was unable to document a single instance where a child completed a suicide as a result of not being given transing medical interventions.[23]

Dr. Kevin Stuart, Executive Director of the Austin Institute for the Study of Family & Culture, reports, "[M]ultiple studies have shown that over the long run, those who transition have increased rates of suicidality, not decreased."[24]

In fact, there is growing evidence that providing gender-confused children with puberty blockers and cross-sex hormones increases the risk of suicide.[25]

The American Association of Suicidology, in collaboration with numerous other groups, has important recommendations for how the media should cover stories involving suicide because suicide to prevent it from becoming a social contagion. When children see reports of suicide, they are more likely to consider suicide an option. Studies show that suicide attempts go up when media coverage of suicide increases. Dramatic headlines and repeated coverage increase the rate of suicides, and the American Association of Suicidology cautions the media to be careful in how suicide is reported: "The way media cover suicide can influence behavior negatively by contributing to contagion, or positively by encouraging help-seeking."

When trans-rights activists insist that children will kill themselves if not granted everything they demand, they generate a self-fulfilling prophecy because their rhetoric increases the likelihood that children will kill themselves. This is not a subject to be taken lightly. Transgender activists throw "suicide" around like a paper airplane, desensitizing people to what it means.

To understand the suicide claims, it is important to look at both the motivation and the evidence of those claiming that children who are not affirmed will kill themselves.

The motivation is clear: Activists are using suicide to scare parents, health-care providers, teachers, and politicians into supporting their agenda. It isn't children who benefit from being transed. It is big pharma and the industrial medical complex that is benefiting by making billions.

It is unconscionable that activists are willing to make outrageous claims about suicide without any evidence, but that is exactly what they are doing.

Activists propagate wild lies about transing interventions being "lifesaving medical treatment" when, in fact, the data shows exactly the opposite.

There is not much research about the long-term outcomes of medical transitioning, but the research shows that those who identify as transgender have a far higher suicide rate than the general population, that medical transitioning does not cure gender dysphoria, and that those who identify as transgender have high rates of anxiety, depression, autism, and trauma.

Based on the claims of the transgender activists, either medical transitioning increases the suicide rate, or those who identify as have significant underlying issues that increases their suicidality. Either way, it is clear that transitioning does not reduce suicide risk.

The National Suicide Prevention Lifeline
800-273-TALK (8255)

Recommendations for Reporting on Suicide:
https://www.datocms-assets.com/12810/1577098761-recommendations.pdf

RESEARCH

This section is not just a definition of research, but it's dedicated to debunking the pseudo-research transgender activists use to support their claims.

Transgender activists will often dismiss anyone who disagrees with them as a *science-denier* when, in fact, they are the ones who are bastardizing science in order to justify their ideology.

The Federal Drug Administration (FDA) was established to protect people, and ensure that drugs and medical interventions are safe and effective. Most people assume that any medical intervention prescribed by a health-care provider has been studied and approved by the FDA, or equivalent oversight in other countries; however, there is a loophole.

One which transgender activists have exploited.

Drugs and other interventions can be prescribed for what is called *off-label use*. Though the intervention has been approved for some uses, a health-care provider can prescribe it for a condition or population it has not been approved for. For example, there are just two antidepressants that have been approved for treatment of depression in children under the age of eight years old: fluoxetine (Prozac) and escitalopram (Lexapro).[26] Sometimes doctors will prescribe other antidepressants that have been used in teens or adults for young children, even though the drug has not been tested or approved for use in young children. The dosage, side effects, and long-term consequences of using the drug on young children with depression has not been studied, and are not known.[27]

Off-label use of puberty blockers and cross-sex hormones is how health-care providers have been able to offer unproven and damaging medical interventions to treat children struggling with gender dysphoria.

Dr. Patrick Lappert notes using puberty blockers and cross-sex hormones is "not even accepted by the FDA and no one has done a clinical trial, not one clinical trial to even demonstrate the safety" of using these drugs on children.[28]

***

Due to previous violations of human rights by unethical researchers, there are guidelines that must be followed when doing research on people. The guidelines are even more strict for research on children.

The side effects and potential negative outcomes of interfering with a healthy child's endocrine system are potentially so catastrophic, it is unlikely that any researcher could get approval to study the efficacy of puberty blockers and cross-sex hormones on children with gender dysphoria.

The widespread use of unapproved medical interventions to treat gender dysphoria is akin to the heinous medical experiments performed by unscrupulous researchers prior to the development of protections for research participants.

Ironically, the best way to treat gender dysphoria—and the only proven treatment—is either doing nothing and allowing a child to naturally progress through puberty (sometimes called *watchful waiting*), or watchful waiting combined with talk therapy.[29]

Treating a condition that overwhelmingly resolves over time with off-label drugs is bad enough, but the use of puberty blockers, cross-sex hormones, and mutilating surgeries that cause irreversible harms is unconscionable.

Even health-care providers who prescribe these interventions admit that there is not enough known about these them. Dr. Robert Garofalo from the Center For Transgender and Sexuality at Lurie Children's Hospital in Chicago says, "We don't know with regard to some of the long-term consequences of these medications [puberty blockers and cross-sex hormones]. If you look at our consent forms, they are fraught with vague language and like 'may' and 'could.' We know very little about things that are really important to families like fertility, like cancer potential or oncologic potential of these agents, cardiac risk."[30]

Dr. Michelle Cretella sums it up: It is "a massive breach of medical ethics."[31]

Transgender activists make wild assertions that transgendering medical interventions are not just necessary, but lifesaving.

Looking at the so-called *research* that activists use to support their assertions show these declarations are not just misleading, blatantly false.

In addition to unfounded claims that transing a child will reduce the risk of suicide, the limited research that has been published, primarily by transgender rights activists, has major methodological flaws.

- **Studies are focused on those who medically transitioned as adults**

Activists argue that children should be medically transitioned, but they are using research based on adults to support claims that children will commit suicide if not allowed to medically transition. This is problematic for a number of reasons, the biggest being that research shows that up to 97% of children will outgrow gender-dysphoric feelings if allowed to naturally progress through childhood. Studies from adults who continue to suffer from gender dysphoria into adulthood cannot be generalized to children because the adults who still suffer from gender dysphoria represent a tiny fraction of children who suffer from gender dysphoria. It means that up to 97% of children are being given the wrong treatment in order to address the small percentage who will continue feeling gender-dysphoric into adulthood.

Another problem with using adult studies is that children are very different physiologically than adults, especially children who have not gone through puberty. It is common knowledge among health-care providers that adult treatments cannot be randomly applied to children. Children's brains and bodies are developing and growing and therefore, medical interventions that might be helpful for adults can be devastating for children.

- ## Studies focus on the experiences of gays and lesbians

Transgender activists have been incredibly successful at hitching their wagon to the LGB movement, even though the LGB movement is based on sexual orientation, which is not even tangentially related to gender dysphoria. It is true that some gays and lesbians are gender nonconforming and therefore may develop gender dysphoria. It is also true that some gays and lesbians are encouraged to transition in order to appear straight. However, analyses being used to support the trans activists are not about the experience of gender dysphoria of gays and lesbians. Instead, research exclusively about the experiences of gays and lesbians are being substituted for those who identify as transgender. An example is Caitlin Ryan's study about the impact of so-called *conversion therapy*. In addition to having a number of other methodological flaws, Ryan's research, though cited by transgender activist, is about gays and lesbians.[32] Ryan's and other studies like hers have been used by activists to suggest that if children with gender dysphoria are not allowed to medically transition, they will commit suicide—a gross misuse of research results.

- ## The studies are not longitudinal

The "honeymoon effect" is well known for those receiving medical treatments, especially cosmetic surgeries.[33] When someone initially accepts medical care, even if it isn't a good treatment, patients often report feeling better. However it isn't because the treatment is effective—it is because of the patient's hope and desire to feel better, and belief that the intervention will help. After the honeymoon is over, patients often experience depression and other worsening mental-health issues when they realize the remedy didn't prove as effective as they hoped.

Dhejne, who conducted one of the few longitudinal studies on subjects with gender dysphoria, noted a significant increase in suicidality within ten years of transgender surgical interventions.[34]

There are no long-term studies to show that puberty blockers combined with cross-sex hormones is safe, but the studies available about the long-term use of puberty blockers shows they have debilitating side effects.

- ## The studies' participants are self-selected

One of the hallmarks of good research is that subjects are randomly selected. In all too many studies presented by transgender activists, subjects are recruited in ways that systematically target those who are sympathetic to the results the activists are seeking. They contact self-identified transgender groups and ask for volunteers, or post requests for volunteers in online forums for those who identify as transgender. Results from any survey where the respondents are self-selected are biased.[35]

- ## The data is from surveys that rely on self-reports without any external verification

A survey is just a questionnaire with nothing to confirm the accuracy of responses. There is nothing to prevent those filling out the surveys from lying or presenting misinformation. When respondents are recruited from a biased group, the likelihood of inaccurate responses goes up. When a "study" doesn't require any validation of information provided by subjects, it cannot be generalized to other populations. In addition, surveys are often written in a way to elicit specific responses, so while surveys can be interesting, they should not be considered scientifically rigorous, and the results should be viewed with skepticism.[36]

- ## Surveys are retrospective reports

Most of the surveys that have been done by transgender-rights activists are *retrospective*, meaning the person filling out the survey has to recall things from the past. Retrospective reporting has some significant flaws. Memory expert Elizabeth Loftus has done considerable research showing that memory is flawed and malleable.[37] Recollection without verification of memories results in inaccurate data.[38]

- ## There are no control groups

One of the hallmarks of research is having a control group. A control group allows researchers to determine if an outcome is related to an intervention or not. Many of the studies cited as evidence of the benefits of medical transitioning had no control group.[39, 40, 41, 42] Without such a group of subjects, it can be almost impossible to connect an intervention to an outcome.[43]

- ## Perspectives of detransitioners are not included

Detransitioners are an important population that should be included in studies about medical interventions for those with gender dysphoria. Instead of including detransitioners, transgender activists often dismiss and disparage the experiences of those who formerly identified as transgender.[44]

- ## Data does not take into consideration the positive affirmation and attention participants got from transitioning

Those who adopt a transgender identity are often celebrated at school, home, and by important adults in their lives. They are told they are brave and authentic, while being encouraged to believe that transitioning will cure them of the difficult feelings they have. Most children would show signs of improved mental health if they were celebrated and provided attention. In addition, children who adopt a transgender identity gain a lot of power, as they are allowed to dictate how others address them and treat them.

- ## Studies suffer from significant dropout rate of participants

Loss to follow-up is a term that is used to describe when a study loses participants. For example, if a study started out with 100 participants but ended up with 50, that would be a significant loss. Any loss to follow-up can compromise the results of a study;

however, the higher the loss, the more results need to be questioned. Anything higher than 20% poses serious threats to validity.[45]

The high rates of loss to follow-up in many of the studies cited by transgender activists is shocking. For example, commonly cited studies such as Rehman's had 40.4% loss to follow-up.[46] Ruppin's had 49.3% loss to follow-up.[47] Pimenoff had 56.7%,[48] and van der Sluis lost more than half, at 62.5%.[49] Lindquist had a shocking 69.5% loss to follow-up.[50] These are stunningly high dropout rates by participants, and results from studies with such high rates of loss to follow-up are not valid.

- **Studies make claims not supported by data**

In an ideal world, researchers would only make conclusions and claims based on their data. But increasingly, activist researchers make wild claims which their data does not support.

For example, after the article "Reduction in Mental Health Treatment Utilization Among Transgender Individuals After Gender-Affirming Surgeries: A Total Population Study" by Richard Bränström, Ph.D., and John E. Pachankis, Ph.D. was published, a correction was issued after other researchers analyzed Bränström and Pachankis' data and found their conclusions were not supported by their data. Bränström and Pachankis originally claimed their research showed clear benefits of surgical transitioning.[51] The article was reposted on August 1, 2020, correcting their claim and including an addendum referencing the postpublication discussion captured in the Letters to the Editor section noting that the study actually found that "neither 'gender-affirming hormone treatment' nor 'gender-affirming surgery' reduced the need of transgender-identifying people for mental health services."[52] Though the results from this study have been used to support medically transing children, it did not include any children as subjects. In addition, it failed to look at those with gender dysphoria who did not engage in medical transitioning. Another significant failure by the researchers, they failed to include data about completed suicides by participants, even though it was available. Rather than bolster claims of the benefits of medical transitioning, this research showed the opposite.

Another study often used to support medically transitioning children is the Dhejne study, even though this one actually found a dramatically higher rate of suicide among those who surgically transitioned.[53]

- **Terms are not well defined**

One of the most confounding aspects of most studies that claim to show that medical transitioning children is beneficial is the lack of clarity of terms. In high-quality research, terms are clearly defined so that there is a common understanding of what is being studied. In a formal debate, the first thing the two teams do is to go over definitions of all important words so they know exactly what they are debating.

Terms like *conversion therapy*, *affirmative care*, and *transgender child* are often used in research without being defined. This is especially problematic in surveys. For example, a study might ask participants if they have ever been suicidal. Some might answer yes if suicide has ever entered their thoughts, whereas others might not answer yes to this question unless they had a plan to carry out a suicide attempt. The term *conversion therapy* has been applied to the idea of electrocuting someone to force them to change their sexual attraction, and to a parent who will not use the pronouns a child requests. These are drastically different interpretations of the term.

- **Dosages for puberty blockers and cross-sex hormones are not controlled or consistent**

There is no specific guideline for the dosages of puberty blockers and cross-sex hormones for children. This can undermine the validity of any research about medical transitioning. Some children might be on high doses of puberty blockers and cross-sex hormones as part of their transing, while others may be on milder doses. The experiences and outcomes of those on puberty blockers and cross-sex hormones will depend, to some extent, on dosages.

- **Small sample size**

The sample size of a study needs to be large in order to achieve generalizable results. Many studies have thousands of participants, while numerous studies used by trans activists have very small sample sizes. The smaller the sample size, the greater the risk of error, and the less generalizable and valid the results are. Commonly cited studies by trans activists such as O'Bodlund's had only twenty-three participants,[54] van der Sluis had only nine[55] and Sørensen only eight.[56] These are incredibly small studies and the results cannot be applied to others struggling with gender dysphoria.

One of the more recent surveys that has gained national attention and is being used by transgender activists to bolster their position is Jack Turban's survey.[57] Turban's survey has so many methodological flaws, it is shocking that Assistant Secretary for Health Dr. Rachel [Richard] Levine, in the United States Department of Health and Human Services, cited it as evidence that giving puberty blockers to gender-dysphoric–children reduces suicide.

Dr. Levine tweeted on January 24, 2020: "A new study has found that Transgender youth with access to a puberty blocker have decline[s] in chances of suicide + mental health problems now and in the future. This study is important because it's the first to show this specific association."[58]

This indicates that either Dr. Levine has not actually read Turban's study, or that he does not understand basic research methodology. Either way, it suggests that Dr. Levine should not be in a position of advising anyone about health care.

It is unfortunate that the US Assistant Secretary for Health perpetuated the unsubstantiated myth that puberty blockers and other transgender medical interventions reduce suicide in children by citing such profoundly flawed research. But this is right out of the playbook of transgender activists.

Among the methodological flaws of Turban's research, Turban conducted a survey, not a study. The results don't actually show a reduced risk of suicide among children given puberty blockers. It fails to acknowledge that puberty blockers induce a developmental delay in otherwise-healthy children. In addition, the way in which

Levine and others discuss Turban's results may, in fact, increase the risk of suicide among children with gender dysphoria because suicide can be a social contagion.

Here are some other problems with Turban's survey:

- The survey asked adults if they wished they had received puberty blockers, but it did not actually look at the long-term consequences of children who were prescribed puberty blockers
- Participants were recruited online and were not representative of the overall population[59]
- Participants were recruited through transgender advocacy organizations, and subjects were asked to "pledge" to promote the survey among friends and family; this recruiting method yielded a large but highly skewed sample [60]
- The survey results were based upon interviews, with no corroboration of claims made by those who were interviewed
- The survey failed to associate even one suicide in a child not getting puberty blockers
- The survey fails to consider that those who identify as transgender have higher rates of depression, anxiety, and suicidal ideation compared to their peers[61]
- Those who reported taking puberty blockers had double the rate "for serious (resulting in inpatient care) suicide attempts in the year preceding the data collection,"[62] suggesting that adults who took puberty blockers were at a higher rate for suicidality
- The survey looked at relatively short-term experiences of those who had been prescribed puberty blockers[63]
- Of those who took puberty blockers, almost two-thirds were adults when they started taking them, so they do not capture the experience of children taking puberty blockers, especially prepubescent children[64]
- This survey didn't include the experience of any detransitioners[65]

Turban's survey was "compromised by serious methodological flaws, including the use of a biased data sample, reliance on survey questions with poor validity, and the omission of a key control variable, namely subjects' baseline mental health status." Thus, Turban's conclusions are not supported.[66] And yet, this survey is cited over and over again by media outlets and activists. Even more disturbing, some trans activists are claiming that they don't need evidence that transing those with gender dysphoria is safe and effective.

Physician Katie Imborek admits that there isn't evidence for the use of medical interventions to treat gender dysphoria, and that it is "paternalistic" to have an expectation that medical interventions be supported by research. Stef Shuster, a transgender activist, says that "evidence based medicine" isn't needed when treating those with a transgender identity.[67]

Sexologists Michael Bailey and Ray Blanchard conclude, "[T]there is no persuasive evidence that gender transition reduces gender dysphoric children's likelihood of killing themselves."[68] And no study has shown that any medical intervention has a better success rate for resolving gender dysphoria than simply allowing a child to progress naturally through puberty. No study has proven that any medical intervention for treating gender dysphoria is effective.

The quality of research used by transgender activists to justify the use of medically transitioning children is riddled with methodological flaws. Unfortunately, few media outlets take the time to vet research, and therefore often perpetuate dangerous and spurious claims.

TYPES OF TRANS

"In times of universal deceit, telling the truth is a revolutionary act."

~ George Orwell[69]

The media, activists, and even schools talk about *transgender* or *trans* as if anyone who adopts a trans identity is a poor soul trapped in the wrong body, and who is suffering due to the disconnect.

In fact, there are many different reasons someone identifies as transgender. In order to fully understand the ideology, it is important to understand the divergent reasons people adopt a transgender identity.

Not Always Gender Dysphoria...

Autogynephilia (aka AGP)

Dr. Ray Blanchard noted in a Twitter tweet that "Autogynophiles' anger toward women results from envy of women and resentment at not being accepted by woman as one of them."[70]

Many men who want to present as women are sexually aroused by imagining themselves as women. It isn't that they are distressed by not presenting as feminine, it is that imagining themselves as women gives them sexual pleasure, and often they get a thrill and sense of power by infiltrating women's sex-based spaces. It is difficult to know if someone is an AGP or if they are actually suffering from gender dysphoria, or if they are a pretender, predator, or profiteer (discussed later in this section). One giveaway in identifying an autogynophile is his unrelenting and unwavering insistence that he "is a woman."

he autogynophile, in his very insistence that he is a woman, reveals that he has no understanding of what it is like to be a woman.

Autogynophiles are motivated by sexual arousal. It isn't uncommon for an AGP to become aroused at the sight of a used tampon (some go so far as to rummage through the garbage for used pads and tampons, which they then wear), or to insist that he has periods because he "is" a woman. Some even claim to have menstrual periods, or that a nosebleed is how they menstruate.

An especially disturbing illustration of how autogynophiles have insinuated themselves into the mainstream is a video made by a teenager girl called, "How to simulate a period (for transgender women)."[71] This video has a disclaimer at the beginning, saying, "Menstruation is something natural that is constantly associated with being a 'woman,' therefore it is completely normal for all women to want to experience this sensation and I hope you can all appreciate that."

This teenager has clearly bought into the idea that it is possible for a man to become a woman simply by saying he is one, and that we should do everything within our power to accept him as a woman.

Assistant Secretary for Health Rachel Levine, formerly known as Richard, married, had children, and then claimed he is a woman. For Richard, being a woman means presenting with a regressive stereotypical look, such as long hair and lipstick. He is not a woman, he is doing his best to impersonate a woman while those around him support his appropriation of womanhood.

Some autogynophiles have surgery to alter their body and some don't, though most choose to keep their male genitalia because part of their fetish is being aroused by looking like a woman. Because they are aroused at the idea of being a woman, they often desire breast augmentation.

As one former AGP says, "I am a boob guy and like boobs, so whenever I get the urge to touch a boob, I can just touch my own."[72]

The Three Ps: Profiteers, Pretenders, and Predators

Anytime a man is accepted as a woman, or a woman is accepted as a man, it provides deceptive role models for children. This can lead them to believe that they can become something that they are not.

In the past, transexuals were accepted as males who preferred to appear more feminine, and women who preferred to appear more masculine. The transgender ideology insists that people who claim to believe they feel like the opposite sex, both sexes, neither sex, or something else entirely, are actually what they believe themselves to be. This allows any male to demand a right to access women's facilities, sports, and claim any other opportunity reserved for girls and women.

Profiteers

It is not loving or kind or compassionate to undermine women's and girls' rights and protections.

There are individuals who will use whatever advantage they can to profit financially. This might be men who pretend to be women to take advantage of women-only opportunities, or those who are identifying as transgender in order to adopt a "marginalized" category in order to benefit at work, school, or in other situations.

Emilia Decaudin is a man who was elected to a position specifically designated for women in New York's Assembly District 37.[73] He can be seen in a picture taken the night he was elected in a tight dress that clearly shows the lump of his male genitalia. Men like Decaudin, who want to impersonate women, are able to qualify for scholarships and grants specifically set aside for girls and women.

Ute Heggen, in her book *In the Curated Woods*,[74] talks about how her former husband adopted a transgender identity and then took advantage of a government program to promote businesses that had women in leadership roles.

Scholarships, grants, and other opportunities have been set aside for women in order to address the inequality in business ownership, business leadership, and participation in STEM fields. Profiteering men are capitalizing on self-ID to appropriate these opportunities.

Pretenders

Ideally sports will move toward more modest, sex-neutral uniforms, but until then, if a man wants to wear the uniform typically worn by female athletes, it can be argued that he should be allowed to do so while keeping sports fair as he competes against other men.

Unfortunately, men who were mediocre male athletes are increasingly adopting a transgender identity in order to compete against women, gaining what even transgender activists will sometimes grudgingly admit is an unfair advantage.

In an interview I did with Dr. Timothy Roberts, a transgender-rights activist, doctor, and researcher, he acknowledged that even after having male hormones suppressed and taking female hormones, men retain a significant advantage over women in athletics.[75] Despite conceding to the unfair advantage, activists like Dr. Roberts will insist that it is still fair to allow men to compete as women because transgender individuals are marginalized and oppressed, and there are not very many of them. This kind of thinking is so convoluted that it is difficult to follow, but it is par for the course when it comes to the ways in which transgender activists justify what is clearly unfair.

Just a few examples...

Will (Lia) Thomas, who was a mediocre male competitor, broke NCAA records after claiming to be a woman. His female teammates were forced to share their locker rooms and showers with him, even though he is a fully intact male.[76]

Gavin (Laurel) Hubbard, like Will Thomas, was a mediocre competitor in men's sports, but took a spot on the New Zealand Olympic female weightlifting team away from an indigenous woman.[77]

Terry Miller and Andraya Yearwood in Connecticut won first and second place in a girls' high-school track meet after claiming to believe they felt like girls, taking two spots away from girls competing in regional championships.[78]

A man will not overcome a woman in competition 100% of the time, but it is undeniable that men have an unfair advantage over women in most sporting events. In addition, men present serious risks to other women when they compete in female contact sports, like rugby or wrestling.

Predators

There are men who will take advantage of whatever opportunity they can in order to prey on vulnerable women and children. They have no hesitation about pretending to be a woman in order to gain access to women's sex-based spaces.

As prisons succumb to the transgender ideology, we are increasingly seeing hard-core criminals, like Douglas Perry, moved into women's prisons. Douglas, a "violent male serial killer who murdered three prostituted women, is currently being housed at the Washington Correctional Center for Women after securing a transfer under recent self-identification laws."[79]

Predatory men are emboldened to violate women's safety and privacy by entering locker rooms and gym showers. Darren Merager was outed as a male when he entered the women's locker room at the Wi-Spa in California. Cubana Angel, a brave woman who was infuriated at Merager's behavior, recorded herself as she complained to the front desk about the man who was in the women's locker rooms. Rather than her concerns being addressed, Angel was mocked by onlookers and told by the front desk attendant that the spa allows men who say they are women to violate the woman's locker room and showers.

Angel's concerns were 100% valid, as it turns out. "Law-enforcement sources revealed that Merager is a tier-one registered sex offender with two prior convictions of indecent exposure stemming from incidents in 2002 and 2003 in California."[80]

Any man who enters women's bathrooms, locker rooms, and showers is violating women's rights and privacy, and thereby, the very act reveals a predatory nature.

Gender Dysphoria

Gender dysphoria is having discomfort with one's biological sex. Those who struggle with gender dysphoria have a deep-seated desire to kill who they are and recreate themselves as someone else.

Men with gender dysphoria do not fetishize women's spaces or appropriate women's sports, nor are they dangerous predators. Rather, they have extreme discomfort being male and are attempting to opt out of manhood in order to find relief.

Gender dysphoria used to be far more commonly diagnosed in men. This could be because it was more acceptable for masculine girls to be called *tomboys*, or dismissed as having penis envy, whereas society was less tolerant of effeminate boys. Girls who wore pants and played sports were simply "boyish," but boys who liked skirts and tea parties were "sissy," "weak," or somehow less of a man.

Gender dysphoria can be caused by a myriad of underlying issues, including but not limited to:

- Internalized misogyny/misandry
- Internalized homophobia
- Depression/anxiety
- Sexual assault/abuse
- Trauma
- Autism
- Eating disorders
- Pornography

Internalized Misogyny/ Misandry

In a reddit post, a young woman wrote about how internalized misogyny was causing her gender dysphoria, saying, "I keep feeling like the ENTIRETY of my experience of 'womanhood' is… Suffering. And there's nothing positive about it. Everything people tell me is supposedly positive about womanhood makes me feel worse." She went on to say that she'd want to be a woman in a "non-sexist space."[81]

Girls and woman, boys and men are being told that if they don't adhere to regressive sex-based stereotypes, they may not be the sex they were born. It isn't surprising so many children and young adults are rejecting these stereotypes by adopting a transgender identity; however, by doing so, they are reinforcing the very sex-based stereotypes they are rejecting for themselves, and setting off an avalanche of gender confusion. The more the transgender ideology is accepted, the more people will believe they are transgender, and the more these regressive stereotypes define what it means to be male or female.

Internalized Homophobia

Detransitioner Sydney Wright has become an important voice for lesbians. She says it was internalized homophobia that caused her to adopt a transgender identity. "In my mind, the people that were the transgenders, they were walking the streets with their girlfriend or loved one. Nobody knew that they were actually gay."[82]

Effeminate boys and masculine girls may develop gender dysphoria because of their parents' fear that a gender-nonconforming child indicates the child will be same-sex attracted. Believing that sexual attraction is defined by external stereotypical behaviors and preferences, homophobic parents may prefer a child who appears straight and encourage the child to identify as transgender.

Kai Shappley's mother, Kim Shappley, admits in a documentary that she was terrified that her son might be gay simply because he did not adhere to regressive sex-based stereotypes about how boys are supposed to act. She said, "We started praying fervently," and that she even searched the internet for information about conversion therapy.

When she learned about "trans kids," suddenly her gay boy was no longer gay, but a girl born in the wrong body.[83]

Depression/Anxiety

Trans activists often suggest that the reason those with gender dysphoria experience depression and anxiety is because they are not living as their "authentic" selves. According to this line of reasoning, a person becomes their authentic self by creating a fake identity. In fact, depression and anxiety are likely reasons why someone with gender dysphoria wants to run away from who they are and create a new persona.

In addition, cross-sex hormones likely help alleviate feelings of depression and anxiety in the short term.

Testosterone is a controlled substance, and any woman who takes it will initially get a boost in energy, confidence, and libido. It isn't surprising that girls and women who have struggled with depression and anxiety feel like their trans identity is the solution to their difficult feelings.

Men who take estrogen have reported feeling calm and content. Hacsi Horvath, a man who, in his own words, "masqueraded as a woman" for many years, said taking estrogen was like having a glass of wine.[84]

To complicate matters, medications that are used for depression and anxiety often short-circuit a teen's sexual development. As other young people are having their first twinges of sexual desire, teens on antidepressants and antianxiety medications may either not develop a sex drive, or find that their previously developing sex drive has shut down.

Parents might feel an understandable sense of relief that they needn't worry about their teenagers becoming sexually active, but sexual development is an integral part of human development. Derailing sexual maturation does no service to the young person.

Kids who don't experience sexual interest might feel like they are even more different from their peers, exacerbating the problem further. In addition, there is a large body of evidence that suggests that going through puberty helps alleviate feelings of gender dysphoria. When a child's natural puberty is undermined by psychotropic medications, it can sabotage the very mechanism that can be curative.

Sexual Assault/Sexual Abuse

It makes sense that sexual abuse and assault would cause someone to reject their sex. I identified as a boy after being sexually assaulted. I realized after years of therapy that I was only presenting as a boy in an attempt to keep myself safe from another sexual assault. Because the men who assaulted me focused on my female genitals and ignored my brother, I became convinced that it was my body's fault that they hurt me. The trauma from the assault resulted in me dissociating (a feeling of leaving my body), and when I returned to my body, I returned believing I was a boy.

Kids have incredibly creative coping skills and rely on adults to uphold reality and help them process trauma. Nearly every formerly transgender-identified woman I have interviewed reports either experiencing a sexual assault/abuse, or the desire to flee her body after unwanted sexual attention.

It is not surprising that boys also respond to sexual assaults and abuse by developing gender dysphoria. Often boys experience an erection when being sexually traumatized and direct their anger and shame over the assault at their genitals. Billy Burleigh, who was sexually abused by his swim coach, says the first thing he asked when waking up after his vaginoplasty was, "Is it gone?", meaning, was his penis removed?

His transgender identity was a rejection of the male genitalia that betrayed him during the abuse.[85]

Trauma

There are many kinds of trauma that can cause someone to reject themselves and desire to become someone new. Divorce, bullying, or having an abusive parent can all cause dissociation. When someone dissociates, they are primed for the transgender ideology that tells them the discomfort they have is due to being born in the wrong body. For someone who is already struggling to feel connected to themselves, this provides the perfect explanation. Becoming someone new allows them to recreate themselves as the person they want to be, rather than having to process the difficulties they have endured. It is very much like putting a bandage over a festering wound.

The wound is covered up, but the infection doesn't go away.

Autism

Children with autism are increasingly encouraged to believe they are transgender.

In her article "12 Causes of Gender Dysphoria," Melinda Selmys observed, "Women with Asperger's and other autism spectrum conditions often report that they find it easier to interact with males, and to fit in in male society. Some of the common symptoms of autism (lack of social awareness, a tendency towards more logical forms or abstracted forms of thought) may be experienced as 'masculine.' Autistic people are also often asexual and may have a complicated relationship with their bodies. On a purely anecdotal level, I've found that gender-atypical presentations seem to be more common with autistic friends than among neurotypical folks."[86]

One clinician at a gender clinic reported the concern, "Maybe we're medicating kids with autism."

Rather than performing a full diagnostic assessment of children who came to the clinic, it was assumed that the children were transgender if they experienced gender dysphoria.[87]

One autistic detransitioner from the Female Detransition and Reidentification study said, "My autism made me see other females as a completely different species."[88]

Ashira, who was diagnosed with autism after she detransitioned, said, "I think that as a kid, it was difficult for me to communicate in general, in terms of, like, my feelings and my inner world could not communicate. So having some way to identify what was wrong was a reason that I, what do you call it, turned to transgenderism."[89]

According to the Center for Disease Control, about one in fifty-four children has been identified with autism spectrum disorder.[90] Yet the rates of kids being transed who are on the autism spectrum is outrageously higher. The study, Clinical Presentations and Challenges Experienced by a Multidisciplinary Team and Gender Service, found that nearly 14% of the children being transed were diagnosed with autism. Considering that boys are four times more likely to be diagnosed with autism than girls, but more girls were represented in their study, this is an alarming rate.[91] It is likely the rates of autistic children being transed is even higher, as many girls with autism go undiagnosed.

Eating Disorders

Children with eating disorders and other types of body dysmorphia can also experience feelings of gender dysphoria. This shouldn't be a surprise, since eating disorders result from blaming one's body for one's problems. This excessive focus on the body results in a generalized dysphoria and a disconnect between the body and the mind.

People suffering body dysmorphic disorders feel like they are in the wrong body. As one detransitioner wrote, "I confused my body dysmorphia, brought on by the pressure to be thin, small and beautiful and worsened by my anorexia, with dysphoria. I thought that the only way I could be happy being large and strong and obnoxious and taking up space was by being male."[92]

Doctors would never agree to perform liposuction or a gastric bypass on an anorexic patient who is convinced she is fat, but will chop breasts off anorexic girls and women who identify as transgender.

Pornography: Boys

Graham Lineham, writer of popular TV shows *The IT Crowd*, *Black's Books*, and *Father Ted*, wrote an article about sissy-hypno porn, saying it "typically involves men wearing lingerie and engaged in 'forced feminization'—eroticizing the illusion of being made to 'become women' through dress, makeup, and sexual submissiveness, and the fetishizing of the humiliation this brings."[93]

Boys and young men are having their sexuality highjacked by pornography. Though it may be difficult to see these overly sexualized boys and men as victims because their behavior is unnerving, they are in need of support to help them reclaim both their sexuality as well as their identity as male.

Pornography: Girls

More than ever before, billboards, TV shows, and movies portray women as sexual objects.

It is not surprising that in our hypersexualized culture—where pornography depicts women being spit upon, choked, and forced to lick urine off the floor—many girls want to run away from womanhood.

One detransitioner said the biggest reason for her desire to be a man was that "the boys at school wore normal clothes. But the girls sported short shorts, crop tops, sexy leggings, and swooping cleavage. On TV, you see footage of Met Gala or the Oscars and all the men are wearing modest suits, but all the women are wearing spandex dresses that barely cover their nipples and nothing else. I thought, 'if this is womanhood, I don't want any part in it.'"[94]

Rapid-Onset Gender Dysphoria (ROGD)

ROGD is the development of a reported discomfort with biological sex that comes on quickly around puberty and may be triggered by feeling the discomfort all youth feel with the changes brought on by puberty.

In her study, "Rapid-onset gender dysphoria in adolescents and young adults: A study of parental reports," Lisa Littman found that "Rapid-onset gender dysphoria (ROGD) describes a phenomenon where the development of gender dysphoria is observed to begin suddenly during or after puberty in an adolescent or young adult who would not have met criteria for gender dysphoria in childhood. ROGD appears to represent an entity that is distinct from the gender dysphoria observed in individuals who have previously been described as transgender."[95]

Abigail Shrier's exposé *Irreversible Damage* explains how girls with rapid-onset gender dysphoria are being encouraged to transition, rather than being taught to manage the difficult feelings associated with adolescence. As Shrier says, "The psychological struggles that lead a young woman to transition are often acute."

She also notes that "the new 'affirmative-care' standard of mental-health professionals is a different matter entirely. It surpasses sympathy and leaps straight to demanding that mental-health professionals adopt their patients' beliefs of being in the 'wrong body.'

"Affirmative therapy compels therapists to endorse a falsehood: not that a teenage girl feels more comfortable presenting as a boy— but that she actually is a boy."[96]

Gender Nonconformity

Those who do not adhere to regressive stereotypes about how someone of their sex is supposed to look, act, think, and feel will often be told by transgender activists that they are transgender. The message is that children who are gender nonconforming will be happier and healthier as adults if they transition as children, forgo normal puberty, take hormones to force their body to develop sex characteristics of the opposite sex, and finally undergo invasive surgical procedures that eliminate sex organs of the opposite sex and confer fake sex organs.

Transhausen by Proxy

There is a psychiatric condition called Munchausen by Proxy whereby parents crave the attention they get from having a child in need of medical interventions. Those suffering will often intentionally harm their child.

The term *Transhausen* is being applied to parents who appear to meet the criteria for Munchausen by Proxy, but get the attention they crave by manipulating their child into believing he or she is transgender. Since so many of these parents are mothers, another phrase often used is *munchie mom*.

Parents with Transhausen are energized by the attention they get from having a transgender-identified child.

In addition to craving attention, which is a hallmark of Munchausen by Proxy, Transhausen parents push their children to believe they are the opposite sex for other reasons, such as:

- A parent's discomfort with a gender-nonconforming child
- A parent's disappointment about the sex of a child
- A parent's desire for a child of the opposite sex
- A parent's desire to profit from a child's trans identity

Parents of transgender-identified–children often garner praise and personal profit by telling the story of his or her child. The stories center around the parents and their perceived virtues for being so loving and affirming of their child.

Social Contagion

Psychologist Jill Glover observed, "Current pediatric gender transition is very much a social contagion. It is a fad fueled by current sex ed curriculum in schools, by Hollywood and our entertainment industry by social media, as you've already discussed, and a deliberate attempt to profit financially from destruction of our children by certain activist groups and those who would target the innocent and impressionable, our youth are experiencing higher rates of anxiety, depression, and other mental health disorders."[97]

Both Lisa Littman and Abigail Shrier found that often, one girl announces a transgender identity, and within days, her friends were also claiming a transgender identity.

A detransitioner says an acquaintance told her that "our whole friend group was just us all slowly realizing we're gay, and now it's just us all slowly realizing we're trans."[98]

In her article "Inside Planned Parenthood's Gender Factory," Shrier reports concerns of clinicians who were seeing girls arriving in groups and giggling in the waiting room together. This is not indicative of children struggling with gender dysphoria, but instead, a group of girls who have been infected with a social contagion.[99]

Critical Theory

Another one of Littman's findings was that children who ascribed to a neo-Marxist view of privilege were far more likely to develop rapid-onset gender dysphoria.

She noted that critical theory, which is often introduced to elementary school children under the guise of tolerance and diversity, teaches that those who are heterosexual, white, and don't identify as transgender "are considered evil and unsupportive, regardless of their actual views on the topic. To be heterosexual, comfortable with the gender you were assigned at birth, and non-minority, places you in the 'most evil' of categories with this group of friends."[100]

The parent of a detransitioner told me that her daughter reported discussing who was marginalized, and it was clear that being a *cis-het* (cis-gender heterosexual) white girl was not going to cut it. As such, she was considered one of the oppressors. Her daughter realized that if she identified as transgender, she would flip from being an oppressor to being a victim.

It isn't surprising that white, middle-class children who would otherwise be considered the most privileged (or in their minds, most evil) have a desire to opt out of their identity as an oppressor.

Transing allows them to change from being considered the oppressor to being marginalized and oppressed.

***

It is unimaginable that we are transing children with dangerous and experimental interventions, rather than helping them learn to manage their difficult feelings. In none of these cases is someone who identifies as transgender "born in the wrong body," and there is no evidence that it is beneficial to allow or encourage anyone to impersonate the opposite sex. Ever. There is a tsunami of evidence that allowing people to impersonate the opposite sex is harmful.

TREATMENT ISN'T AN IDENTITY

There are many treatments for gender dysphoria. Transitioning is the only one in vogue now, despite there being no evidence to support it as either safe or effective.

Unfortunately, therapists, due to ideology or ineptitude, often direct a gender-dysphoric–patient to transition. Hearing the disordered thoughts of a person with gender dysphoria, therapists affirm their feelings of being inherently flawed and urge these troubled patients to create a fake persona.

These people are not innately transgender. Transitioning is a treatment, not an identity.

Many of us who are fighting for better mental-health services for children who suffer from gender dysphoria bristle at the idea of there being "true trans"—unfortunate souls for whom their gender was mistakenly put in the wrong body.

We do not accept that there is a gender spirit that can inhabit the wrong body.

Transgender activists have picked up on our concern and accuse us of trying to deny transgender people's existence. They say we are trying to erase those who are transgender.

What they are forgetting is that transitioning is a treatment, not an identity.

No one is intrinsically transgender.

Someone can identify as transgender and decide to change their appearance to more closely match the opposite sex, or try to nullify their appearance to appear androgynous, but that does not mean they are, inherently, transgender.

There are a few who claim to benefit from treating their gender dysphoria by dissociating from themselves, but these are not individuals who are transgender. They are individuals suffering from a profound mental illness who have been told by health-care providers that their body is so wrong—their very being is so wrong—that the only way to navigate life is to kill who they are and cultivate a new identity.

We should all be enraged that anyone is told that they are so damaged that the only solution is to become another person.

What are the interventions that so many trans activists are claiming to be *lifesaving treatment*?

Below are accounts of *gender-affirming care* described by a number of detransitioners. The first is by Ritchie (aka Tullip), a man who was encouraged to believe he was a woman.

> I have no sensation in my crotch region at all. You could stab me with a knife and I wouldn't know. The entire area is numb, like it's shell shocked and unable to comprehend what happened, even 4 years on.

> I tore a sutra [suture] 4 days post recovery, they promised to address it, i begged them in emails to fix it, they scorned me instead. Years later, I have what looks like a chunk of missing flesh next to my neo-vagina, it literally looks like someone hacked at me. They still wont fix it

> No one told me that the base area of your penis is left, it can't be removed—meaning you're left with a literal stump inside that twitches. When you take Testosterone and your libido returns, you wake up with morning wood, without the tree. I wish this was a joke

> And if you do take testosterone after being post op, you run the risk of internal hair in the neo-vagina. Imagine dealing with internal hair growth after everything? What a choice... be healthy on Testosterone and a freak, or remain a sexless eunuch.

> And thats something that will never come back and one of the reason why i got surgery. My sex drive

died about 6 months on HRT and at the time I was glad to be rid of it, but now 10 years later, Im realising what im missing out on and what I won't get back.

Because even if i had a sex drive, my neo-vagina is so narrow and small, i wouldn't even be able to have sex if i wanted too. And when I do use a small dilator, I have random pockets of sensation that only seem to pick up pain, rather than pleasure.

Any pleasure I do get comes from the Prostate that was moved forward and wrapped in glands from the penis, meaning anal sex isnt possible and can risk further damage.

Then theres the dreams. I dream often, that I have both sets of genitals, in the dream I'm distressed I have both, why both I think? I tell myself to wake up because I know its just a dream. And I awaken into a living nightmare.

In those moments of amnesia as I would wake, I would reach down to my crotch area expecting something that was there for 3 decades, and it's not. My heart skips a beat, every single damn time.

Then theres the act of going to the toilet. It takes me about 10 minutes to empty my bladder, it's extremely slow, painful and because it dribbles no matter how much i relax, it will then just go all over that entire area, leaving me soaken [soaking].

So after cleaning myself up, I will find moments later that my underwear is wet—no matter how much I wiped, it slowly drips out for the best part of an hour. I never knew at 35 I ran the risk like smelling like piss everywhere I went.

Now i get to the point where im detransitioned and the realisation that this is permanent is catching up with me. During transition, I was obsessive and deeply unwell, I cannot believe they were allowed to do this to me, even after all the red flags.

I wasn't even asked if I wanted to freeze sperm or want kids. In my obsessive, deeply unwell state they just nodded along and didnt tell me the realities, what life would be like.

And finally, theres dilation, which is like some sort of demonic ceremony where you impale yourself for 20 agonising minutes to remind you of your own stupidity.

This isn't even the half of it. And this isn't regret either, this is grief and anger. Fuck everyone who let this happen.

When I lost 1600ml blood during surgery, it took days to get a blood transfusion. The surgery lasted 3 hours longer. They joked about the blood loss too.[101]

An account by Scarlet, a young man who was encouraged to believe he was born in the wrong body as a young teenager:

They started me on hormones. And that was within three or four therapy sessions. I was 13 years old, almost 14 when I went on hormones. I was 14 years old when I got my puberty blocker implant in my arm.

So after seeing the gender therapist, I would try to see other therapists, but they wouldn't really talk to me about my confusion or anything like that. And when I talk about my past, because I was already transitioning, they wanted to frame everything around me being trans.

So I couldn't really explore the root of anything, which was why I went to the therapist. I wanted to understand why I had this discomfort. I didn't really want to jump into everything right away. I had never really understood the idea of gender identity, because for me more just like, well, I have feminine mannerisms and I like guys.

So it just makes more sense for me to be pretty right.

The whole time I was going through this, like I would ask them, "what are the side effects of this?" And like, they told me that the puberty blocker was completely safe that there are no adverse side effects. After I was on it for awhile. It, like, castrates. You stop developing in every way, including mentally and emotionally. And it was like being frozen in like a child's body.

On the blockers I had I'd lost muscle, like severe muscle atrophy. I felt frustrated because it was like being trapped in a child's body. So like your sexuality functions differently, like it, you don't really get aroused. I was told that I would be sterile and you know, I was already gay, so I was like, "well, I'm going to adopt anyways," you know, with things not maturing correctly and possibly even atrophying. So then even if I go back, I would have to live my life as a eunuch. It's the exact awkward existence that I was trying to avoid as a feminine gay guy. But it was presented as the only option.[102]

An account by Sydney, a young woman who started testosterone as a teen:

I was on hormones for exactly a year. I've been off now for a year and a half. So one of the effects of the hormones that I'm still living with, there are many that I still do live with, but one of the effects is the deeper voice. It's something I will never probably be able to change. I wished I could, you can't come back from this. My voice has changed forever. I don't know if I'm going to have kids. My body is probably still a little shape masculine from all the testosterone rearranging. And there are just many changes that come from it that you would never expect. The opposite sex hormones are not healthy for you. Your body was not built for that. And putting that on your body, it will cause much more harm.[103]

An account by Chloe Cole, who was put on puberty blockers and cross-sex hormones, and had her breasts removed, as a young teenager:

> I am a 17 year old de transitioner from the Central Valley. I was medically transitioned from ages 13 to 16.
>
> My parents took me to a therapist who affirmed my male identity and the therapist did not care about causality or encouraged me to learn, to be comfortable with my body. He brushed off my parents' concerns about the efficacy of hormones, puberty, blockers, and surgeries.
>
> My parents were given the threat of suicide as a reason to move me forward.
>
> My transition, my endocrinologist, after two or three appointments, put me on puberty blockers and injectable testosterone.
>
> At age 15, I asked to remove my breasts.
>
> My therapist continued to affirm my transition. I attended a top surgery class that was filled with around 12 girls. That thought they were men. Most of my age were younger. None of us were going to be men.
>
> We were fleeing from the uncomfortable feeling of becoming women. I was unknowingly, physically cutting off my true self from my body irreversibly and painfully, our trans identities were not questioned. I went through with surgery despite having therapists and attending the top surgery class.

I really didn't understand all of the ramifications of any of the medical decisions I was making. I wasn't capable of understanding, and it was downplayed consistently. My parents on the other hand were pressured to continue my so-called gender journey with a suicide threat. I will never be able to breastfeed a child. I have blood clots in my urine. I am unable to fully empty my bladder. I do not yet know if I am capable of carrying a child to full term.[104]

Abigail Shrier outlined the irreversible harms that result when children are indoctrinated into the transgender ideology.[105] It is important to understand that adopting the transgender ideology is not a benign declaration of identity—it is damaging to children, both emotionally and physically.

MEDICAL TRANSITION

"Being in a minority, even in a minority of one, did not make you mad. There was truth and there was untruth, and if you clung to the truth even against the whole world, you were not mad."

~ George Orwell[106]

As the testimonies in the previous chapter illustrate, medical transitioning is incredibly invasive. The end result is permanently damaging what was previously a healthy body.

Transing a child starts with allowing a child or teen to adopt exaggerated, stereotypical behaviors and dress often associated with the opposite sex. As the child nears puberty—as young as eight years old—parents are coerced into giving their child puberty blockers with threats that if they fail to do so, the child will commit suicide.

Puberty blockers halt a child's normal physical and mental maturation. They induce a developmental delay, retarding an otherwise-healthy child.

After a child has been on puberty blockers, parents are led to give their child cross-sex hormones: testosterone for girls and estrogen for boys.

Girls as young as eight years old are given both puberty blockers and testosterone, which will render her sterile if she is on this cocktail of hormones long enough to masculinize her body. As both Ritchie and Scarlet noted, puberty blockers, especially in combination with cross-sex hormones, also result in loss of sexual function. Children are consigned to a life without sexual pleasure before they have even experienced a sexual relationship.

There are numerous stories of teens prescribed cross-sex hormones after just one appointment at a gender clinic.[107]

Gender-confused girls as young as thirteen get radical mastectomies to remove their breasts. Both boys and girls as young as sixteen have surgery to alter their genitals.

Transgender activists will often insist that social transitioning is harmless, but it puts a child on a pathway toward, what Abigail Shrier so aptly named her book about the transgender craze, irreversible damage.

Puberty Blockers

Puberty blockers don't only prevent physical maturation, they also inhibit emotional maturation. Children who have been taking puberty blockers are developmentally younger than their peers. They are consistently shown to be less emotionally mature, intellectually retarded (meaning slowed or behind their peers), and developmentally delayed.

The effects of puberty blockers are not reversible. [108, 109]

A child can never recapture the time missed while peers are developing normally. [110, 111]

Dr. Paul Hruz, a professor at Washington University School of Medicine; Lawrence Mayer, a scholar in residence at Johns Hopkins School of Medicine; and Dr. Paul McHugh, of Johns Hopkins University School of Medicine authored the article "Growing Pains: Problems with Puberty Suppression in Treating Gender Dysphoria," which raises serious concerns about the use of puberty blockers for children with gender dysphoria.

Though proponents of puberty blockers say that the effects are reversible, Hruz, Mayer, and McHugh found that "there are virtually no published reports, even case studies, of adolescents withdrawing from puberty-suppressing drugs and then resuming the normal pubertal development typical for their sex." [112]

The long-term side effects for a child taking puberty blockers are unknown.

No research exists because this intervention is so new.

Research on the short-term side effects of puberty blockers include loss of bone density, early-onset menopause, joint pain, and cognitive delays. [113, 114, 115, 116, 117, 118, 119]

One study done in England showed that children taking puberty blockers had an increase in behavioral and emotional problems, self-harm, and suicidal thoughts. [120]

Dr. John Gueriguian, who spent twenty years reviewing drugs for the FDA, stated in federal court papers that AbbVie, the manufacturer of Lupron—a commonly used puberty blocker—intentionally suppressed information about the danger associated with the use of Lupron. [121]

The FDA has an adverse-events database that lists more than 25,000 adverse events associated with Lupron, including suicidal thoughts, vision loss, excruciating pain, and death. [122]

Another huge concern is that the known side effects of puberty blockers are based on relatively short-term use, generally less than three years. A child who announces a transgender identity at eight and is put on puberty blockers will likely remain on then until 14–16 years old. In some cases, children are remaining on them into adulthood.

There is no research into such long-term use of puberty blockers on children who start taking them at the beginning of puberty, but the side effects from short-term use are deeply concerning.

Common known side effects of short-term use of puberty blockers include:

- Redness, burning, pain, and bruising at injection site
- Hot flashes
- Increased sweating
- Night sweats
- Tiredness
- Headache
- Nausea
- Diarrhea
- Constipation
- Stomach pain
- Breast swelling or tenderness

- Acne
- Joint/muscle aches or pain
- Trouble sleeping
- Vaginal discomfort/dryness/itching/discharge
- Vaginal bleeding
- Swelling of the ankles/feet
- Increased urination at night
- Dizziness
- Weakness
- Chills
- Clammy skin
- Itching or scaling
- Testicle pain
- Impotence
- Depression
- Increased growth of facial hair
- Memory problems

In addition to all the risks associated with puberty blockers, giving children puberty blockers encourages them to believe they were born in the wrong bodies, and greatly increases the likelihood these children will want cross-sex hormones and cosmetic surgeries.

Dr. Michael Biggs, a professor of sociology at Oxford, found that not only did almost all the children treated with puberty blockers at the Tavistock Gender Identity Service in the United Kingdom go on to cross-sex hormones, but children taking puberty blockers had an increase in self-harming behavior.

Hruz, Lawrence, and McHugh note that "Gender identity for children is elastic (that is, it can change over time) and plastic (that is, it can be shaped by forces like parental approval and social conditions)." Therefore, puberty blockers interfere with the natural processes by which children become comfortable with themselves.

Once a child starts on puberty blockers, the child is on a pathway to cross-gender hormones.

Side effects of masculinizing hormones for girls:

- An abnormal level of lipids in the blood
- Worsening of an underlying manic or psychotic conditions
- Producing too many red blood cells (polycythemia)
- Weight gain
- Acne
- Developing male-pattern baldness
- Sleep apnea
- Elevated liver function tests
- High blood pressure
- Type 2 diabetes
- Infertility
- Extreme uterine pain
- Uterine atrophy, often necessitating a hysterectomy

Side effects of feminizing hormones for boys:

- Blood clots
- High levels of triglycerides
- Gallstones
- Weight gain
- Elevated liver function tests
- Decreased libido
- Erectile dysfunction
- Infertility
- High potassium levels
- High blood pressure
- Type 2 diabetes
- Cardiovascular disease

Children as young as eight years old are currently being given cross-sex hormones, often in conjunction with puberty blockers, which leave them not only developmentally delayed, but frequently sterilized with a loss of sexual function.[123]

We will not know all the negative consequence of a healthy child taking puberty blockers and cross-sex hormones for decades, but preliminary reports from children who have taken this combination of drugs is shocking. Not only will there be profound damage from these medical interventions, but damage also done to children who are pushed away from the reality of how they were born.

As Dr. William Malone so aptly stated, "[I]n every other aspect of medicine if the mind and the body are misaligned, if the mind is at odds with material reality, biological reality, or some other reality, we do everything we can to get that individual back to foundational reality. But in this situation, we're essentially changing the body to match the brain."

He goes on to add: "We have to agree that there is some fundamental reality that we exist and operate in, and that we can identify that reality with our senses and measurements and agree upon that reality that XX and XY cells are different and they respond differently to hormones. Once we agree upon that reality, if someone is at odds with that reality, we need to help them back to reality, not keep them away from reality."[124]

Unfortunately, transgender activists are pushing children away from reality to dysfunction.

UNDERSTANDING THE THREAT

"For, after all, how do we know that two and two make four? Or that the force of gravity works? Or that the past is unchangeable? If both the past and the external world exist only in the mind, and if the mind itself is controllable—what then?"

~ George Orwell[125]

Indoctrination

An *ideology* is a belief system.

Trans activists either believe, or claim to believe, that children can mysteriously be born in the wrong body.

They believe humans have some kind of gender soul or spirit.

They believe the solution to difficult childhood feelings is to dissociate from oneself and create a fake persona.

They believe that it is okay to use suicide threats to manipulate others.

These are all beliefs.

Like faithful cult members, trans activists either do not realize, or do not care, that their beliefs are based in mysticism and faith, rather than truth and science.

Like some of the most heinous cults of the past, they are actively grooming everyone in our society to accept their beliefs, but they are especially targeting children.

Protecting your child from the trans ideology is much like preparing for an impending natural disaster, such as a hurricane. You know the storm is out there. You have some time to prepare, but not a lot of time because the storm could build strength and hit at any moment. You can't stop it, but the more you know about it, the better you can prepare.

Recruitment

Vulnerability

Because the transgender ideology has infiltrated nearly every aspect of our society, all children are vulnerable to being recruited; however, based on both well-known cult tactics as well as reports from former believers in the transgender ideology, there are some children who are more vulnerable.

Children who have suffered trauma, especially sexual trauma, are particularly vulnerable.

Trauma often results in dissociation, and those who dissociate are less moored to their body. They often feel like they are stuck in a *meat suit*, or in the case of those who have experienced sexual trauma, a body that betrayed them.

Dissociation feels like the self is leaving the body. Children who struggle with feeling separate from their body and who dissociate are at an increased risk of recruitment by any cult, but they are especially vulnerable to the transgender ideology that suggests these feelings are the result of being born in the wrong body, instead of acknowledging that these are well-documented effects of trauma.[126]

In addition to children who have been traumatized, there are others who are more vulnerable to being indoctrinated into the transgender ideology.

Those who have recently moved into a new school or neighborhood and are hungry to fit in. Children who struggle with social interactions, especially kids on the autism spectrum. Children who don't feel strong connections with their family. Children with other mental-health issues. All of these children are more vulnerable to being recruited into the transgender ideology.[127]

Love Bombing

Once a vulnerable child has been identified, the next step in recruitment is *love bombing*. The term comes from the cult called the Unification Church, otherwise known as the Moonies.[128] The Moonies were taught to shower someone they identified as a potential member with love.

Petra, a former trans-identified teen, was an autistic middle-school student who was struggling socially. She was invited to the Gender and Sexuality Alliance Club. As soon as she started attending, she was showered with attention and affection and affirmation.

The closer she moved toward accepting the transgender ideology, the more she was celebrated.[129]

Love bombing feels good.

For many, it can feel like the long search for one's tribe is over. It can feel like stumbling into a family that wants you and loves you even more than your own family. And it isn't just peers who love bomb—adults get in on the action as well. They will call themselves *glitter moms*. If children's families don't support the transgender ideology, the children are encouraged to find *glitter families*.

One of the common memes that appears in social media is "If your parents aren't accepting of your identity, I'm your mom now."

If you search the internet for this phrase, you can find t-shirts, posters, stickers, and even mugs stamped with this saying.

Love bombing goes hand-in-hand with another component of recruitment: Isolating children from those who don't embrace the transgender ideology.

Isolation

Part of the love bombing process is to separate children from those who love them. As children are being love bombed, they develop loyalty for those are showering them with affirmation, affection and attention.

Children are told that anyone who doesn't accept the transgender ideology is hateful and intolerant.

This begins the process of indoctrination.

Children become convinced that those who are love bombing them love them more than their family. They are told that anyone who disagrees with the ideology is a bigot and hateful.

The message is clear: "We love you in a way no one else does."[130]

The child's family is replaced with a glitter family.

Transgender activist Rachel McKinnon posted on social media, "I want you to know that's it's ok to walk away from unsupportive or disrespectful or even abusive parents. And I want to give you hope that you can find what we call your glitter family. Your queer family. We are out there. And the relationships we make in our glitter families are just as real, just as meaningful as our blood families."[131]

Coincidentally, as I was writing this section, Advocates Protecting Children received what is an all-too-typical message anyone fighting the transgender ideology get. This is one of the nicer ones, since it doesn't include threats of rape or torture, profanity, or suggestions that we are Nazis.

"You people are quacks. Scary. You promote scary stuff. Disgusting. If any one of you have a transgender child, send them my way. I will accept [them] for who they are, not what you want them to be."

Conversion

Once a child has been drawn into the ideology, the next step is conversion.

Believers in the transgender ideology want full converts: children who adopt a transgender identity.

Because the trans umbrella is so wide, nearly any child can be convinced that they fit under it; however, it isn't hard to convince

vulnerable children that they are not just queer or questi
that they were born into the wrong body.

Tried and true cult techniques are deployed to move children into full allegiance to the ideology.

Memory Manipulation

Elizabeth Loftus has done groundbreaking work on memory. She and others have shown that our memory is incredibly malleable.[132]

As part of the conversion process, children are encouraged to question their past as they are given the message that being trans will solve all their problems. The foundation of the transgender ideology is built on regressive sex-based stereotypes. If children, at any point in their lives, didn't conform 100% to these stereotypes, it is presented as evidence that they are transgender.

A girl plays with toy trucks? Transgender.

A boy enjoys flowers? Transgender.

The emotion attached to memories of nonstereotypical behavior is then gently manipulated.

Children start to attach strong feelings of contentment and happiness to the memories they have when they were acting in nonstereotypical ways, and the memory is used as proof that the child was always transgender.

If a child doesn't have any clear memory upon which transgender activists can draw, Loftus also found that it isn't that difficult to create false memories.

Transgender activists exploit the difficult emotions all children feel as they grow up, and pin those emotions onto a false narrative. As this is done, children are coached to remember past difficulties relating to not conforming to sex-based stereotypes, resulting in the child's history being rewritten.

It is incredibly damaging to suggest to children that regressive sex-based stereotypes determine if someone is male or female; however, children—especially vulnerable children who are starved for acceptance—will believe outrageous ideas in order to fit in.

Again, since virtually all children have engaged in activities that are not stereotypical for their sex, and all children struggle with difficult feelings, it is easy to convince them that all those difficult feelings are due to being born in the wrong body.

Identity Manipulation

Once a child accepts that they are transgender, the ideology insists they create a new identity. They are encouraged to essentially kill who they are and create a false persona.

This creation of a new identity is the linchpin in the conversion process.

Children are taught that when they were born, the doctor guessed at their sex and got it wrong. That their parents were confused in mistaking them for the wrong sex. That all their life, everyone got it wrong...including themselves.

The only way to remedy this error that began the moment they were born is for them to become their "authentic" selves by becoming someone else.

This creates an incredible loop of confusion. Who they thought they were is wrong. They have to embark on a *gender journey* to discover who they really are. Becoming who they really are requires them to become someone new.

The use of puberty blockers, cross-sex hormones, and surgery are presented as important steps on the gender journey but they are, in fact, initiation rites designed to fully indoctrinate children.

Reality Manipulation

True believers in the transgender ideology are convinced that identifying as transgender is the only way to happiness. All too often, detransitioners will talk about each step they took to feminize or masculinize their appearance.

It starts with a social transition.

Social transitioning involves taking on stereotypical charac-teristics of the opposite sex. For girls, it means a haircut, a new wardrobe, and, if puberty has started, breast binding. Girls sometimes put a fake penis—what looks like a sex toy—in their panties to simulate the bulge of a penis. For boys, social transitioning means a name change, long hair, and often overly glittery and ruffled pink and purple clothes. Boys are often encouraged to "tuck" their penis. This involves either pushing the penis and testicles into the abdomen, or taping the genitals between the legs so they are less obvious.

Next comes medical transitioning.

Puberty blockers for children as young as eight years old.

After puberty blockers come cross-sex hormones, and often surgery.

Each of these steps toward building a new identity confuses reality. Children who are in environments where they are affirmed in their new identity have to grapple with suppressing who they are and staying in character as their new persona. They are urged toward each successive stage with celebratory enthusiasm, each action making them somehow more authentic in the eyes of those who believe in the ideology.

Those who are not affirmed by important people in their lives are encouraged to view themselves as being victims of hatred and abuse. These children are given the message loud and clear: The only way they are lovable is if they become someone new.

Thought Manipulation

Thought stopping is one of the techniques that can be used to get out of a cult, to improve one's life, or to modify behavior in a positive way. For example, when I struggled with gender dysphoria, I learned to pay attention to my thoughts, and when I started telling myself that I was a boy, I would intentionally stop the thought and redirect myself to remember that I was suffering from gender dysphoria as a result of a sexual assault. Doing this reminded me where the thought that I was a boy was coming from, and why. Over the years, I learned to stop the thought quickly and replace it with more positive thoughts, such as, "The sexual assault was not my fault," and finally, to encouraging thoughts such as "I am a strong and capable woman."

Transgender activists, like other members of other cults, use thought stopping in a nefarious way. It teaches children to accept the ideology without question and to respond to challenges in ways that stop them from questioning the ideology.

An example of a cascade of thought stopping starts with "Trans women are women." If someone asks, "What is a woman?" the response is "Anyone who identifies as one." Instead of taking time to process and consider someone's questions, they are immediately labeled as hateful and pushed away so the transgender activists don't have to think critically.

The ideology teaches that anyone who does not accept this nonsensical response is a hateful bigot.

A few more examples:

Q: "What is a transgender child?"

A: "Any child who says they are transgender is transgender."

Q: "How do you know if you are transgender?"

A: "If you feel transgender, you are transgender."

Q: "What does it mean to feel transgender?"

A: "Transgender feelings are valid."

Q: "Why do I have to affirm my child's transgender identity?"

A: "Would you rather have a trans child or a dead child?"

Q: "Why should men be allowed to compete in women's sports?"

A: "Trans women are women."

Q: "Why should children be given puberty blockers and cross-sex hormones?"

A: "Don't erase trans kids."

Q: "Don't puberty blockers retard development?"

A: "Puberty blockers are fully reversible."

Q: "If all kids who say they are transgender are transgender, how do you account for detransitioners?"

A: "A detransitioner was never really transgender." Or, "A detransitioner has been taught to suppress who they are and is only pretending to be happy."

Q: "If gender is innate, how is it also fixed and fluid at the same time?"

A: "Everyone has a different gender journey."

Any pushback on the thought-stopping responses results in accusations of being a hateful, transphobic bigot, a TERF, and sometimes even a fascist or Nazi.

There is also a whole language of trans, some of which was discussed in the first chapter. The trans language is used to undermine reasonable thought and foster confusion. This keeps converts off balance and unable to think critically about the ideology.

***

In addition, the ideology encourages use of emotional appeals that are patently absurd.

In an interview with Matt Walsh in his documentary "What is a Woman?", gender doctor Michelle Forcier responds to Walsh's attempt to establish that a chicken that lays eggs is a female chicken by saying "Does a chicken cry? Does a chicken commit suicide?"[133]

A chicken's ability to cry or commit suicide has nothing to do with it being male or female, but Forcier was attempting to derail Walsh's line of inquiry because she was unwilling to answer a simple question.

Is a chicken who lays eggs female?

Othering

One of the hallmarks of cults is using language that makes it clear who is "in" and who is "out."

As mentioned above, those who push back on thought-stopping responses are labeled as haters, transphobic, bigots, abusers, fascists, TERFs, and ironically, Nazis.

Nazis used *othering* to manipulate the people of Germany to perpetrate the horrors of the Holocaust. Many Nazi supporters refused to believe that Jewish concentration camps existed; they insisted that Jews were only being deported. In the same way, people who have capitulated to transgender ideology refuse to believe in anything that threatens their beliefs.

Children are taught that anyone who doesn't affirm them is hateful and trying to ease their existence. Such hateful people are less than human.

In another trick of language, the transgender ideology claims to promote inclusion and tolerance...while being intolerant of anyone who disagrees, and treating them as less than human.

Othering is used to dehumanize naysayers, and ultimately can be used to justify not only cutting off all contact with anyone who doesn't accept the transgender ideology, but in some cases, doing bodily harm to them. Some transgender activists advocate rape, torture, brutality, and murder of those who disagree with them. [134]

Coercion

As mentioned above, those who are vulnerable to being recruited by transgender activists often have underlying issues.

Transgender activists convince kids who have adopted a transgender identity that it is the identity that will keep them safe, healthy, and even alive. [135]

To convince children that they have to change their external appearance in order to be able to live with themselves is unforgivable. Children should be taught to manage difficult feelings in a healthy manner.

The transgender ideology suggests that a child who struggles with gender dysphoria will commit suicide if not affirmed and given access to interventions that change their outward appearance. They suggest that puberty blockers, cross-sex hormones, and surgeries are "medically necessary" and "lifesaving." This leads children to believe that they need these interventions to stay alive, and anyone who is hesitant to provide them is guilty of attempted murder.

Transgender activists tell newly converted children that if someone misgenders them, or uses their deadname, it is actual violence.

This reinforces the idea that those who believe the transgender ideology are safe and loving, and those who don't accept the ideology are dangerous.[136]

Cult expert Steven Hassen has a number of books about how cults recruit and keep members. Below are a number of other thought-control techniques he has identified that are consistent with the techniques used by transgender activists:

- Require members to internalize the group's doctrine as truth

- Instill black-and-white thinking

- Change a person's name and identity

- Use of loaded language and clichés that constrict knowledge, stop critical thoughts, and reduce complexities into platitudinous buzzwords

- Teaching thought-stopping techniques, which shut down reality testing by stopping negative thoughts and allowing only positive thoughts, including:

    ♦ Rejection of rational analysis, critical thinking, and constructive criticism
    ♦ Labeling alternative belief systems as illegitimate, evil, or not useful
    ♦ Instill new "map of reality"[137]

As disturbing as it is to expose the devious tactics used by transgender activists to indoctrinate vulnerable children into their harmful ideology, knowledge is power. Understanding the transgender ideology, and the way in which transgender activists recruit and attempt to convert children, provides important insights for protecting your family.

Recruitment in Schools

In early September 2017, a kindergarten teacher in Rocklin, California, read the book *I Am Jazz* to her class as part of an announcement to the children that one of their classmates was mysteriously changing sex.[138] The book is about a boy who discovers he was born in the wrong body. Some of the children in the class were disturbed by what happened, and went home expressing to parents anxiety that they too might have been born in the wrong body.[139]

This kind of exposure of young children to transgender ideology in schools might be written off as an anomaly in 2017, but it is increasingly becoming the norm.

Well-funded transgender activists have worked to get books like *I Am Jazz* into every classroom in the country.

On February 28, 2019, transgender activist Tim McBride (aka Sarah McBride) and the president of the National Education Association, Lily Eskelsen Garcia, held a press conference during a kindergarten class at a public school in Arlington, Virginia.[140]

The two read *I Am Jazz* and other transgender-promoting books as part of the Welcoming Schools program, sponsored by the Human Rights Campaign.[141]

McBride tells the impressionable children, "When I was born, the doctors and my parents, they all thought that I was a boy."[142]

The University of Colorado offers a class called "Queering the Schoolhouse" with instructor Jacob McWilliams, Director of the Gender and Sexuality Center at the University of Colorado–Anschutz Medical Campus and Director of the Women and Gender Center at the University of Colorado, Denver.

McWilliams is a woman who has a masculine presentation and uses "he/him/his" pronouns. One of the goals of the class is to teach instructors how to introduce children to transgender ideology. McWilliams says in the course introduction, "It's fine if you don't yet know the language people use to talk about queer and transgender people. Throughout this course, we'll provide you with resources to help you with terminology and key concepts."

A popular provider of comprehensive sexuality education is Advocates for Youth. Despite graphic videos—aimed at what many agree is grooming of young children with explicit sexualized content that encourages reckless sexual behavior—school districts across the nation have welcomed the free curriculum provided by Advocates for Youth into their classrooms. The Rights, Respect, Responsibility curriculum states that children who are transgender "were called a boy or a girl at birth and may have body parts that are typically associated with being a boy or a girl, on the inside, they feel differently."[143]

This is confusing for children to make sense of. Lessons continue to plant the idea into children's minds that they might have been born in the wrong body even if they never noticed before. "If you were to look in the mirror and see your body, what you see in the mirror—what we just discussed—is part of your biological sex. If you were to close your eyes, how you see yourself based on those body parts is your gender identity. In most cases, how people feel when they close their eyes matches what they see in the mirror. This is called being 'cisgender.' You might commonly hear people refer to just being 'male' or 'female,' but the correct term is 'cisgender.' For some people, what they see in the mirror and how they feel on the inside are different. This is called being 'transgender.'"[144]

A student who is being confused about these concepts might talk to a school counselor.

Unbeknownst to parents, school counselors reinforce the transgender ideology. The American School Counselor Association (ASCA) adopted the following policy in 2016 (modified in 2022).

"School counselors promote the use of best practices to inform their support of transgender and gender-nonconforming students."

It is unclear how the ASCA substantiates a claim that "the following are best practices," but these are the policies that are increasingly adopted by our public schools, from kindergarten through high school.[145]

"**Names and Pronouns.** School staff should address students by their chosen/affirmed name and pronouns corresponding to their gender identity, regardless of whether there has been a legal name change."

Yes, this means that a student can identify as candy gender with a chosen name of "Skittles" and pronouns of "sweet/sticky/tart," and the school staff will use this name and pronouns for the child without ever checking with parents for permission.

"**Student Records.** Schools should make every effort to use students' chosen/affirmed names on student records, even if a legal name change has not been made. This includes making changes in the school's student information system, so the affirmed name is the one that appears on most printed unofficial materials (e.g., rosters, diplomas, student IDs, yearbooks, school newspapers, etc.) while the legal name is kept in a segregated, confidential file. If students have not disclosed their gender identity to a parent or guardian and as a result their name and/or gender marker cannot be changed on their student records, their chosen/affirmed name should be noted as a "preferred name" in the system."

Skittles will have "tart's" records changed to correspond with Skittles' chosen name and pronouns.

Note: Skittles may decide to change from candy gender to air gender, with a new chosen name of "Atmosphere" and pronouns of "sky/sun/moon." The school staff and records will accommodate this change, alongside any other changes.

"**Privacy and Confidentiality Regarding Disclosures.** Transgender and nonbinary students have a FERPA-protected right to privacy; this extends to students' gender identity, birth name, sex assigned at birth and medical history. Schools must make every effort to only reveal information about students' gender identity when others have a legitimate educational purpose, which does not include mitigating possible discomfort of others. This right to privacy and prohibition of disclosing students' gender identity extends to students' parents/guardians, with whom schools should work collaboratively, directed by students' comfort about what and with whom to share their confidential information."

As mentioned earlier, "sweet" gets to decide if and when to share that a new identity has been adopted at school. This policy suggests that school staff should actively deceive Skittles' parents if sweet asks them to.

In other words, school teachers, counselors, and even the custodian will be compelled to use Skittles' chosen name and pronouns while actively hiding tart's newfound gender identity from Skittles' parents.

"**Restrooms and Locker Rooms.** Students have the right to use restrooms and locker rooms matching their gender identity. Schools should work with transgender and nonbinary students to ensure they feel safe and can use the selected facilities with dignity."

This means a boy can go into the girls' bathrooms and a girl can go into the boys' bathrooms simply by declaring themselves to have a gender identity that aligns with the opposite sex's bathrooms. Fellow classmates have to accept other children's gender identity. Essentially, the school is saying "accept this lie" to everyone—adults and children alike—at the school.

In addition, girls are at risk of sexual assault when boys are allowed into their bathrooms. In Loudoun County, Virginia, a male student was found guilty of raping two different girls in the girls' bathroom.[146]

"**Physical Education Classes and Intramural Sports.** Students should be allowed to participate in physical education classes and intramural sports aligned with their gender identity."

By suggesting that children participate in PE classes of the gender they identify with, they are not only putting girls at risk during contact activities, such as field hockey or soccer, because males are often more aggressive and have bigger bodies, they also suggest that boys be allowed to shower after participating in PE or sports with the gender they identify with.

"**Interscholastic Sports.** Students should be allowed to participate in interscholastic sports aligned with their gender identity."

In other words, boys should be allowed to compete in girls' sports regardless of the clear competitive advantage a male high-school student has. As with the policy related to PE and intramural sports, boys identifying as girls put girls at risk of injury during team sports, and undermine a girl's right to privacy in showers and locker rooms. In addition, boys who claim the identity of girls undermine the very reason girls' sports were created—to give girls an opportunity to excel in sports while competing on a fair playing field against other girls.

The above policies are not fringe; they are middle of the road.

Some schools have gone so far as to convert bathrooms and showers to "all gender."

In December of 2021, Chicago public schools issued a new policy to make all bathrooms "inclusive." In other words, Chicago schools no longer have bathrooms for boys and girls; rather, any child can use any bathroom.[147]

This experiment was conducted in the UK.

The *Daily Mail Telegraph* reported that parents were raising concerns about one school's move to open up bathrooms to both sexes. One parent noted that "there are seven-year-old girls using the same toilets as 11-year-old boys." After pressure from parents, the school determined it was in the best interest of children to have sex-segregated bathrooms.[148]

Shockingly, the trans ideology is being pushed by the United Nations and World Health Organization. The following is what is taught to children in Eastern and Southern Africa with UNFPA's *Comprehensive Sexuality Education Participant's Workbook.*[149]

"Gender identity is the gender that a person feels themselves to be, regardless of their body. Most of the time, a person's biological sex and their gender identify are the same. In other words, a person with a female body feels and identifies herself as a woman. However, some people feel that they are in the wrong body. They are transgender. Some say that they have a female brain trapped in a male body, or the other way around. Some identify with neither genders; some identify with both genders; while others feel they cannot relate to the idea of gender at all."

***

"Being born in the wrong body" or "having the brain of the wrong sex trapped in one's body" are mystical concepts at best.

For children who still believe in the Easter Bunny, it is planting a dangerous idea that doctors, parents, and teachers might have made a grave error and misgendered them when they were born. And to make matters worse, the only solution offered for those who feel any kind of disconnect from their body is to become a different person, often with the use of puberty blockers that induce developmental delays; cross-sex hormones that, in combination with puberty blockers, cause sterility and loss of sexual function; and finally, elective cosmetic surgeries that remove healthy body parts.

All this, and there is no evidence to support either that it is possible to be born in the wrong body or that feminizing a boy's body or masculinizing a girl's body is a safe and effective treatment for children who have what are the relatively normal difficult feelings of childhood.

DOUBLE SPEAK

"To the future or to the past, to a time when thought is free, when men are different from one another and do not live alone—to a time when truth exists and what is done cannot be undone: From the age of uniformity, from the age of solitude, from the age of Big Brother, from the age of doublethink—greetings!"

~ George Orwell[150]

Confounding Communication

Propaganda

The misinformation children are getting at school is reinforced by news sources. To suggest what is being reported is fake news minimizes what news outlets are doing. They are not making up random stories. They are systematically crafting a narrative using language to manipulate the population's understanding of reality.

The mainstream media reports about men who compete against women in sports as "trans women," and sometimes even just "women."

When bills are introduced that would prohibit men from entering women's spaces, they talk about "Discriminatory anti-trans legislation aimed at trans women."

When schools craft policy requiring children to use the bathroom that corresponds to their sex, headlines read: "Schools banning trans children from bathrooms."

And when sports authorities issue regulations that require men to compete against other men, they claim, "Trans women being banned from sports."

People who are not familiar with the transgender movement believe the headlines without digging deeper.

Some people are under the impression that medical interventions can actually change someone from being a man or a woman.

Many believe that there are just a few very sad and desperate people whom these bills are attacking.

Increasingly, men who claim to be women who are convicted of crimes are covered by the media as if they really are women.

Headlines such as "Woman who sexually assaulted 10-year-old girl as teen will serve sentence in juvenile facility"[151] are common. This story is about a man convicted of sexually assaulting a 10-year-old girl. He now identifies as a woman.

The BBC changed the testimony or a rape victim in coverage of the trial, referring to the rapist's penis as "her penis."[152]

Children are being taught to accept the transgender ideology increasingly younger ages.

For 2022 Pride Month, the big-box store Target focused on toddlers with a "Trans Rights are Human Rights" t-shirt.

Even children's shows like *Blue's Clues* are forwarding the ideology with a cartoon portraying a beaver riding on a float during a Pride parade. It has surgical scars from what is euphemistically called *top surgery*—the removal of otherwise-healthy breasts so that a girl, or in this case, a beaver, looks more like a male.[153]

Disney has changed many policies at its amusement parks, such as the elimination of gender greetings. Park staff no longer say hello to "boys and girls." Instead, staff are instructed to say, "Hello everyone," or "Hello friends."

Many TV shows and movies directed at children have at least one transgender-identified character.

It is near to impossible to shield kids from the ideology.

Though the tsunami of transgender messaging aimed at children is daunting, there are things that parents and caregivers, friends, and family can do to help gird your child so they can reject the ideology.

PART 2: GOING ON THE OFFENSIVE

"Not merely the validity of experience, but the very existence of external reality was tacitly denied by their philosophy. The heresy of heresies was common sense."

~ George Orwell[154]

Healthy families are protective. When children feel loved and supported at home, with clear boundaries and high expectations, they are less vulnerable. Cults know this and specifically target children who are alienated from their families.

Cults also actively undermine families.

This does not mean that all kids who proclaim a transgender identity come from dysfunctional homes (although, truth be told, all families struggle with some degree of dysfunction at times), nor does it mean that every kid who comes from difficult circumstances will fall victim to the trans ideology.

There are ways to strengthen your family—to close ranks to fend off the transgender ideology

ARMING YOUR FAMILY

"It has its private language and its common memories, and at the approach of an enemy it closes its ranks."

~ George Orwell[155]

Reality Grounding

The transgender ideology thrives on undermining reality. Men are women, feelings are fact, and children dictate medical care. One way to fortify your family against the fantasy and fiction of the transgender ideology is to ground your family firmly in reality.

Pictures

One of the goals of the transgender ideology is to undermine a child's history. Creating a home life where children are consistently reminded of their past protects them from attempts to indoctrinate them in the future.

Display lots of pictures of your family.

Put pictures in the kitchen, hallways, living room, bedrooms and even the bathroom. Include pictures from birth to the present. Enlarge pictures showing your family engaging in activities together in loving moments, times that were special for your family.

Pictures of family remind children of their history and give them a sense of belonging.

Reminiscing

Regularly reminisce about past experiences with family. The good times, the silly times—times when your family bonded.

Start this as early as you can.

Encourage each member of the family to take turns telling stories.

Make family stories part of daily routines, such as at bedtime or dinner time.

Reminiscing creates a family narrative that children can draw upon when transgender activists encourage them to rewrite their history.

Build Relationships

Building strong relationships within your family is worthwhile even without the threat of the transgender ideology. But with trans activists on the lookout for vulnerable children, it is even more important.

Snowballing Memories

Creating memories will help instill in children a connection with their family, as well as provide you with pictures to remind children of their family connections and stories to retell. All of these actions will strengthen children's bond to their family.

The concept of snowballing memories is to build upon previous memories. One positive experience gets overlapped with another and another, an ever-growing snowball of history from which the child can draw memories.

These kinds of memories are hard to rewrite because they are anchored to previous experiences and feelings.

As with a snowball, it is almost impossible to remove one layer because the layers become one.

In order to create snowball memories, build upon previous positive memories. If a child remembers a birthday party at a park, host other events at the park and reminisce about previous visits to the park each time.

- If you go on family trips, snowball the memories of those trips.
- Talk about previous trips while planning the next trip.
- Take time during the trip to reminisce about previous trips.
- Point out how the trips are similar or different.
- Have each member of the family talk about what they liked most about previous trips, and connect those experiences to the current trip.

Family Identity

Create family traditions—the more personalized to your family, the better. Have a specific tradition for each holiday and consider creating family holidays. Traditions evoke a sense of nostalgia as children look forward to upcoming holidays.

Create a family journal or blog and have some kind of ritual about how entries are added. Perhaps everyone can have a bowl of ice cream as the journal is passed from person to person, and as each family member makes an entry or reads entries out loud.

Develop personalized ways of showing affection within your family, such as a special family handshake, or fist bump or hug.

The more connected children feel to their families, the harder it will be for a glitter mom to insinuate him or herself in their lives.

Values Clarification

Increasingly values clarification exercises are being used in schools to promote the transgender agenda under the guise of comprehensive sexuality education. For example, the United Nations Educational, Scientific and Cultural Organization (UNESCO) offers an online teacher training course that includes an entire unit on "Values Clarification," including a "Core Comprehensive Sexuality Education Values List."

One of the items on the list is, "Every person's sexual orientation and gender identity is deserving of respect."

Though this might seem harmless, it isn't.

Transgender ideology is presented as fact rather than a belief system. For example, the training states, "Gender Identity: our inner sense of who we are in terms of gender. In most cases, our biological sex matches our feelings, which makes us 'cisgender,' or what most people call 'male' or 'female.' When our biological sex does not match our inner sense of who we are, we are called 'transgender.'

It continues with additional misinformation. "Gender binary is the problematic assumption that there are only two genders (man/male, woman/female), and that they are distinct and unchanging. There is now more awareness of, and support for, the different ways that people identify outside of the gender binary (i.e., genderqueer/gender nonconforming/gender nonbinary). People who do not identify as a man or a woman may identify as both genders, neither gender, between genders, or not gendered at all. Gender does not always match a person's assigned sex at birth, and gender can change over time."[156]

Values clarification in this instance is actually *values manipulation and indoctrination.* Teachers are told that certain values are inherent in comprehensive sexuality education—in other words, it isn't a value at all. It is a belief that is being presented as true.

One of the stated goals of most comprehensive sexuality education programs is to promote values clarification; however, as you can see from the example above, the goal isn't for children to clarify their own values, but rather to be taught falsehoods as truths as part of an indoctrination process.

***

Let children know that values clarification exercises are likely going to be introduced to them at some point. Let them know that this is an attempt to undermine their values, and let them know that it is okay for them not to agree with the misinformation being presented as fact.

Talk with your family about what your values are. Explore w__ your values are important. Identify the consequences of your values in various situations. Role-play situations in which children can put their values into practice.

Values clarification can start at a young age. As you read children's books with your child or watch a TV show or movie, introduce your values. Clarify your family values to your children and then explain how something that happened in the show illustrates why your value is important.

A few important values to consider introducing to children early on:

- People are either male or female
- Males are boys and men, and females are girls and women
- Someone is male or female based on biology, not feelings
- Our outward appearance does not change us from being male to female or female to male
- Not everyone holds the same values, and others will attempt to undermine your values
- If someone encourages you to hide things from your parents, that is a signal to tell your parents immediately

Children who have already thought about their values and had parents help to clarify them at home will be less vulnerable to having their values manipulated by transgender activists.

Skill Building

Personal Grounding Skills

Children are at an increased risk of recruitment into the transgender ideology after trauma, or a significant life change. Parents can't prevent trauma or, for instance, the feelings of isolation a child feels after a move, but there are skills you can teach your children so that they are more resilient when life is difficult.

ı Brewer

ıg *Techniques*

ho have been traumatized, and some children who наvен ι, sometimes feel disembodied. This is a dissociative process, and the result is a loss of connection to themselves. The transgender ideology specifically encourages children to dissociate and view their body as separate from themselves. Children who already dissociate can easily be convinced that the dissociative feelings are an indication that they were born in the wrong body.

Teaching children grounding techniques that they can use anytime they feel stressed or overwhelmed can help them manage difficult feelings. These techniques also draw children back into connection with themselves and their body. Children who employ these techniques will be less likely to feel disconnected from themselves.

If children are already struggling with dissociation, these techniques will help reconnect them with themselves and their body. Anything that draws upon the five senses will help with grounding. Below are some recommendations to get started:

- Breathe deeply
- Cuddle a stuffed animal
- Apply lotion to hands and feet
- Savor a favorite food or drink in a quiet environment
- Smell flowers, vanilla, or another strong and pleasant aroma
- Take a walk
- Go outside and listen for birds
- Take a shower
- Pet an animal
- Make mud pies, garden, or do yard work
- Listen to uplifting or inspiring music
- Do an art or craft project
- Clean a room
- Play a physically active sport or game

Positive Self-Talk

Most people engage in self-talk throughout the day. W
unaware of it, but this internal dialogue can be _____ ~y
transgender activists who introduce unhealthy self-talk to vulnerable
children.

Parents can model positive self-talk to children. In addition,
parents can actively teach children positive self-talk skills. There are
many books about self-talk, but the underlying ideas are all pretty
similar.

Start by teaching children to pay attention to their thoughts and
internal-dialogue. You can help children to be more aware of their
thoughts by asking them how they are feeling, and then, what
thoughts they are having.

Children might struggle to identify the feelings they are having,
but often will be able to tell you what they are telling themselves.
When the self-talk is negative, help the child to find a way to revise
the message they are telling themselves.

For example, if your daughter comes home from school upset
about doing poorly on her test and reports her self-talk is, "I am a
failure," encourage her to change her internal message to, "I am
successful, and my mistakes help me grow" or "I am good
at ____(fill in the blank)."

If your son is telling himself he is stupid because he spilled
orange juice all over himself, help him change his internal dialogue
to something like, "I am good at cleaning up messes."

Changing negative self-talk to positive self-talk helps children
feel more confident and more aware of their emotions. Interestingly,
changing self-talk can also change emotions and improve children's
moods.

Cognitive behavioral therapy is, in part, about teaching people to
rewrite past experiences in a way that is empowering. My therapists
encouraged me to view myself as a survivor of sexual assault rather
than a victim. I was encouraged to view my gender dysphoria as a
creative coping skill rather than as an indication that I was actually a
boy trapped in a girl's body.

Critical Thinking Skills

The transgender ideology is nonsensical.

Children who have good critical thinking skills, especially those who understand common flaws in research design and logical fallacies, will be less vulnerable to recruitment.

As with positive self-talk, there are a lot of books available dedicated to critical thinking skills, but here are few ideas for how to help children grow up learning to think...rather than accepting everything they see as true.

One way for children to become critical thinkers is to critique advertisements. Make it a practice to sit down with your family and look at ads. Figure out the claims that the ads are making and if they are true. If you can't tell if they are true, what information would you need? Where would you get it? Investigate companies in the ads that make claims about being kind and caring. Are they? What techniques do the ads use to manipulate you into wanting to buy their product?

This kind of critique of advertisements can be a fun family activity if it is done in a lighthearted way, but the lesson children learn is to not accept everything they see at face value.

Since the transgender ideology has captured the media, you will have ample opportunities to help your child practice critical thinking skills.

As I am writing this, the national news has announced that Elon Musk's daughter is changing her name and claims she wants nothing to do with her father.

It took a little digging to find out that in fact Elon Musk's *son* has petitioned the court for a gender change and wants to change his name from Xavier to Vivian.[157] I had to look at a number of articles to figure out what the true story was.

This kind of confusing reporting happens regularly in relation to policies about sports, bathrooms, self-ID, medical interventions for gender dysphoria, and therapy bans.

I'd recommend having a copy of WoLF's media style guide on hand, and talk with your family about why the style guide is important and point out how whatever story you are discussing at the time doesn't follow the style guide recommendations.[158]

METHODOLOGICAL FLAWS IN RESEARCH

Because transgender activists misrepresent research results, it is critical that children learn basic research methodology. In a previous chapter I outlined some of the methodological flaws in so the called *research* transgender activists cite to justify their ideological stance. Below I will give you some ideas for you can teach your children to identify flaws in research themselves. Analyzing research can be complicated, but there are concepts about research methodology that can be taught at a relatively young age.

Below are some of the most common flaws with research involving people (who are referred to as *subjects* when participating in research), and some ideas for how to help children learn to spot them.

Applying Results from One Group to a Different Group

Applying results from one group that has been studied in research to a different group is a common way to mislead people about research results. Transgender activists often take research results based on studies involving same-sex attracted individuals and generalize the results to those who identify as transgender.

Sexual attraction is completely different from belief in transgender ideology. Therefore, the results are not applicable to those who struggle with gender dysphoria.

This is something kids can understand easily.

Try doing a poll of all family members about what their favorite dessert is. Once you get the results, make an absurd claim about another family having the same favorite desserts as your family.

Another way to show how ridiculous it is to apply results based on one population to another can be a simple statement such as, "I like apples more than bananas. Everyone likes apples more than bananas."

Encourage your family to explain why that is not true.

Biased Recruitment of Subjects

All too often, studies done by transgender activists recruit subjects from transgender activists' groups. This is biased recruitment of subject and is a flaw in research design.

To help children understand this concept, explain to them that some groups tend to have certain beliefs. Tell them you want to find out what percentage of the population believes in God, and that you will ask everyone at the local church to participate in a survey to see what percentage of the population believes in God. See if your children can spot why this will not provide generalizable results.

This is exactly what transgender activists are doing when they recruit subjects from transgender activists' groups.

Self-Selected Subjects

People who have a strong belief about something are more likely to participate in a study about that topic.

Because of this, good research finds what is called a *representative population*. This means finding subjects that will reflect the larger population accurately.

Since transgender activists often recruit subjects exclusively from groups who believe in their ideology, the results are not valid.

To help children understand this concept, tell your family that you are going to do some research about the best ice cream place in town. In order to do this, you are going to take research participants to three different ice cream parlors, and then ask the participants which has the best ice cream (if your kids don't like ice cream, pick something they do like). Then ask if there are any volunteers. Ask them if they would have been as excited to participate in a study about the best tire store in town. When they show less enthusiasm for assessing local tire stores, explain to them the concept of self-selection and how it skews results.

Unclear Definitions

Reading research done by transgender activists can be incredibly frustrating. They use words that are not defined, or are defined in a way that is not accurate. This is effective because participating subjects are recruited from groups that have bought into the transgender ideology's convoluted and feelings-based language.

One often cited survey of transgender-identified–individuals claims that those who identify as transgender are often denied health care. As it turns out, they are denied elective cosmetic surgery to change their external appearance, something that many agree is not health care.[159] In this case, being denied health care means not getting elective treatments.

Children can be confused by this because they are often unclear about the nuances of language, but you can illustrate how confusing unclear definitions are by saying something like, "It is bedtime" a couple of hours before they usually go to bed. Most kids will balk at this and argue that it isn't bedtime. You can make the case that whatever time you tell them to go to bed is bedtime.

Children have an internal sense of justice and will recognize that you are not being reasonable. This can lead to a discussion of why it is important to have agreed-upon definitions.

Retrospective Self-Reporting

Transgender activists often ask adults who are self-selected subjects, recruited in a biased way, to report on how they felt as children or teens. This is called *retrospective self-reporting,* and it is flawed in two ways.

First, as was discussed earlier, memory is notoriously malleable, and how we interpret and then re-remember our childhood changes as our experiences and beliefs change. Self-reporting about childhood feelings gives insights into how the adult feels about his or her childhood, but does not necessarily reflect accurately how the subject felt during childhood. In addition, there is no verification of what the subject reports.

If a survey asks subjects if they felt depressed during childhood, the subject might project his or her feelings back into childhood. If the participant in the study had a happy childhood but is currently depressed, he or she will focus on the negatives and low points and may taint positive childhood experiences with current negative feelings. Since the very basis of transgender ideology is manipulating past memories and convincing individuals they were born in the wrong body, the memory of subjects who identify as transgender is especially suspect.

One detransitioner says that she purposefully focused on her memories in which she acted stereotypically masculine: her favorite books were about trucks, her love of soccer, and preferring camping to shopping. She dismissed stereotypically feminine activities, labeling them as childishness, and convinced herself that she didn't enjoy them as much as she did at the time.[160]

It is difficult to stage something to illustrate this to children, but often when looking at pictures or talking about past activities together, children will realize they misremembered something. This presents an opportunity to talk about how it is not unusual to misremember sometimes, and why it is important to have pictures, journals, and other ways to remind us of our past.

Limited Time Span

Because the use of puberty blockers, cross-sex hormones, and surgery on children is relatively new, it is impossible to do what are called *longitudinal studies* on outcomes. Children who are put on these interventions initially feel happy because they have been convinced that it is the only way for them to be their "authentic" self. Therefore, asking a child shortly after accessing puberty blockers, cross-sex hormones, or surgery if he or she is happier will not provide important information about how the child will fare over the long term.

Children understand this intuitively when you remind them about how they had a favorite toy that they no longer play with, or a favorite food they no longer enjoy.

When someone in the family mentions a change like this, it is a great opportunity to talk about the importance of thinking in the long term, and how we all change our minds about things on a regular basis.

Failure to Consider Important Variables

Transgender activists refuse to admit that children have difficult feelings for any number of reasons other than the mystical claim that the child was born in the wrong body.

Anytime a study shows that those who identify as transgender have higher rates of suicide, transgender activists will suggest this is evidence that those who identify as transgender should get whatever medical interventions they want, use whatever bathroom they want, participate in whatever sports category they want, and dictate what pronouns others use. However, though it is clear that those who have accepted the idea that they were born in the wrong body have increased mental-health issues, including higher rates of suicidality, transgender activists fail to acknowledge that poor mental-health outcomes could be due to the belief that they are inherently flawed or that they have other mental-health issues.

When children make a general proclamation about something it can be an opportunity to discuss variables. For example, if a child says, "It is going to rain today," explore all the different factors that will influence if it will actually rain. Variables can also be explored when something happens in the world, such as, if you see someone speeding down the street, ask your family why the driver might be speeding.

Consider all kinds of possibilities.

Perhaps the driver is sick and trying to get home. Perhaps a loved one is in the hospital. Perhaps the driver is late for work. Perhaps the car's speedometer is broken, or perhaps the driver enjoys speeding.

Helping children think of various reasons to explain something will help them be more critical when confronted with the false claims made by those who ascribe to the transgender ideology.

***

In addition to being able to understand common research flaws, children also need to understand logical fallacies. Transgender ideology is based on fallacies, and the more children are able to recognize these flaws of argument, the more they can refute claims made by transgender activists.

LOGICAL FALLACIES

Transgender ideology is inherently illogical and inconsistent, so transgender activists have to rely on logical fallacies when defending their beliefs.

Oftentimes these logical fallacies initially seem compelling. The more children can recognize how logic is being distorted to manipulate them, the better equipped they will be to resist indoctrination.

Ad Hominem Attacks

Because the transgender ideology is based on feelings rather than facts, transgender activists will often make personal attacks on those who challenge their beliefs. This is called an *ad hominem attack.*

It is very hard to explain how men suddenly become women simply by saying they are women, so anyone who challenges this absurdity is labeled a hateful transphobic bigot.

This not only derails a reasonable exchange of ideas, but it is also a key component of cultic indoctrination, instilling an "us against them" mentality.

Typically those who employ ad hominem attacks are not interested in a civil exchange of ideas. They are interested in demeaning and discrediting anyone who doesn't accept their beliefs. Ad hominem attacks are deployed by cults to stop members from thinking, and to encourage the belief that anyone who does not accept their ideology is less than human.

Children often use ad hominem attacks simply because they don't have more advanced reasoning skills. If your daughter comes home from school and says something like, "My teacher is stupid for giving me so much homework," point out to her that she has made an ad hominem attack on her teacher, and challenge her to modify her statement. You can help by making suggestions such as: "Calling your teacher 'stupid' is an ad hominem attack. Your teacher isn't stupid, but it sounds like you are upset with your teacher. That doesn't make her stupid, but I can understand that you are not happy about having so much homework."

This kind of restatement does a couple of things.

It lets your child know that name-calling isn't appropriate.

It allows her to reframe her thoughts to address what she is feeling.

It gives her a word for name-calling and an example of how to respond to an ad hominem attack.

When others use ad hominem attacks, discuss it as a family. Children need to understand that just because one person calls another a *bigot* or *Nazi* does not mean it is true, and in fact, it undermines the credibility of the person doing the name-calling.

Strawman

The funny name for this logical fallacy can help you to visualize what it is. Imagine trying to hit a target with a ball, and every time you get ready to throw, a dancing scarecrow jumps out at you. It is hard to concentrate on your target with such a distraction.

A strawman is a dancing scarecrow designed to take your mind off of your target and force you to focus on something else— something often absurd, like a dancing scarecrow!

Transgender activists are pros at using this kind of distraction.

Anytime you hear a claim that transphobes (ad hominin attack) are trying to prevent transgender children from using bathrooms at school, you are seeing a dancing scarecrow. No one is trying to prevent children from being able to use a bathroom, or participate in sports. Reasonable people are suggesting that boys should use the boys' bathroom and participate in competitive sports against other boys, and girls should use the girls' bathroom and compete against other girls.

Transgender activists use strawmen (or to be politically correct, we should rename the fallacy a *person of straw*) to make those who disagree with them look absurd and unreasonable.

Strawman arguments are used because they are effective and difficult to spot.

When I was a child, parents often used a strawman to encourage children to eat all their food. Reluctant eaters were told, "There are children starving in China (or India, or Africa)."

Obviously a child eating his dinner will have no impact on a hungry child in another country, but this kind of emotional manipulation can be effective, even if it is nonsensical.

Point out strawman arguments when someone in your family uses one. Discuss how strawman arguments can be the result of confusion or miscommunication. Sometimes someone thinks your stance is different than it actually is, but often, strawman arguments are intentionally used to make someone look like an extremist or a fool.

False Dichotomy

Another logical fallacy employed regularly by transgender activists is a *false dichotomy*. One of the most common is, "Would you rather have a dead son/daughter or a live daughter/son?"

The idea that a child might commit suicide is horrifying, so a false dichotomy is set up to coerce parents into believing that the only option is to affirm their child.

This false dichotomy is used to manipulate others into believing that there are only two choices, and only one reasonable choice.

False dichotomies can be a powerful form of emotional manipulation. Parents are terrified at the thought their child might commit suicide, so of course many will give in and affirm when they believe there are only two options.

This kind of black-and-white presentation of arguments can be especially compelling to those who are on the autism spectrum, because they naturally gravitate to this kind of thinking. The affirmation/suicide dichotomy is manipulative because it discounts a whole range of other potential outcomes. It is also a dangerous lie.

There is no documentation to support the claim that children who are not affirmed will commit suicide.

This particular false dichotomy is incredibly harmful because it suggests to children who are being recruited by transgender activists that their only choice is for their parents to affirm their newly created identity or to commit suicide.

A false dichotomy is like telling someone that they have to choose A or Z, while neglecting all the letters of the alphabet.

We all know about the letters in between, but children may not have the insight to recognize when they are being misled into believing that there are only two options.

Help children practice identifying alternatives when presented with a false dichotomy.

You can make it fun by joking around with them. If your son's favorite shirt is dirty, suggest "Well, you can wear a dirty shirt or go to school naked."

If your daughter can't find a snack, let her know that she can either go hunt an animal for dinner or starve to death.

Most children will recognize these choices as silly and absurd, but some children on the autism spectrum may not realize you are joking.

These kids need more direct instruction in recognizing false dichotomies, and you might have to sit down with them on occasion and help them brainstorm alternatives to a false dichotomy.

Slippery Slope

A slippery slope argument suggests that once one thing happens, a whole cascade of events will follow, leading to dire outcomes. Slippery slope arguments can be difficult to identify because they start with reasonable assertions.

It can sometimes be difficult to distinguish between a reasonable concern and a slippery slope argument.

A reasonable argument will start somewhere along the lines of, "If A, then B." B is the reasonable and predictable outcome of A.

Slippery slope arguments will say, "If A, then B, C, D, E, F and Z," when Z is a terrible and outrageous outcome.

Often the first few progressions seem reasonable. For example, "If children say they are transgender, other children might bully them."

That is plausible.

Children get bullied for many things—even something as simple as their names—so it is not unlikely a child with a transgender identity might get bullied. However a slippery slope argument would be more like, "If a children say they are transgender, they will get bullied, and we know that children who are bullied become depressed, and if we do not require their classmates to affirm their identity, we will have millions of children dead from suicide."

I have also heard this called *catastrophizing*. Though not all slippery slopes end in a catastrophe, those used by transgender activists often do.

Interestingly, slippery slope thinking is what undoes a lot of New Year's resolutions.

If I decide to give up treats and have a healthier diet, then have a cookie one day, I might think, "Well, I had a cookie today. I will probably have another one and another one, so I might as well just eat whatever I want because I obviously have no willpower at all to eat a healthy diet."

Have fun with your family when talking about slippery slope arguments. You can teach your kids to imagine pushing something down a slide and making a *whooshing* sound whenever someone uses a slippery slope argument.

Circular Argument

Transgender activists use circular arguments to stop critical thinking. One of the most common circular argument used is, "Trans women are women."

When asked, "How can a man be a woman?", activists will respond, "Because they identify as a woman."

In other words, men are women because transgender activists say so, and the definition of a woman is anyone who claims to be a woman.

Many of us would argue that an immutable characteristic such as sex cannot be based on a feeling, but that would be dismissed by transgender activists as a transphobic argument because they have already decided that the definition of a woman is anyone who claims to be a woman.

Another common circular argument is that children who say they are transgender are transgender because gender identity is defined as what children claim their gender identity to be.

It is shocking that doctors are accepting this definition. One of the most influential gender doctors in the country admits that the sole diagnostic criteria for a child being transgender is the child claiming to be transgender.

Dr. Robert Garofalo, Director of the Lurie Children's Hospital, states that when parents ask him to diagnose their children for being transgender he says, "Sure. Ask them. There is no evaluation of someone's gender, it's just a young person who's going to tell you themselves."[161]

If the definition of a transgender child is a child who says he or she is transgender, any child who says he or she is transgender is transgender.

Wow.

I can't think of any other situation where we would ask children for a medical diagnosis and base the diagnosis 100% on the child's self-identification. But in this one case, the medical practitioners who have bought into the transgender ideology embrace these absurd circular definitions.

Arguments based on circular definitions are incredibly frustrating because the definition is flawed. It is essentially someone saying, "I am right because what I think is right is right, and what I think is right is right because I think I am right." There is no room for disagreement or reasonable debate, and this is, sadly, a very common fallacy nowadays.

Encourage your family to spot them when they are used. Children need to be aware that when someone employs a circular argument, it is best to walk away. They are dealing with someone with an entrenched belief who is likely going to try to indoctrinate others, and employ ad hominem attacks against anyone who disagrees.

Appeal to Authority

Transgender activists often say that medical experts support giving children puberty blockers, cross-sex hormones, and surgeries to change their outward appearance. They dismiss anyone who disagrees with them, using ad hominem attacks, and then suggest that their experts are the authorities whose guidance should be respected.

In other words, they are pros at using the logical fallacy of *appeal to authority*. The appeal to authority can be compelling. There are doctors who have bought the transgender ideology hook, line, and sinker. These "experts" are willing to support medical interventions that induce developmental delays, retard growth and development, result in lifelong side effects, and remove healthy body parts from vulnerable children.

The vast majority of people would intuitively recognize that we should not experiment on children with medical interventions that have not been shown to be safe or effective for the treatment of gender dysphoria, but then along comes an expert. The very same people suddenly bow unquestioningly to authority. What people don't realize is that these experts are not unbiased—they are doctors who have either been indoctrinated into the transgender ideology, or are making a huge profit from transing children.

Imagine someone from a cigarette company being called as an expert witness about the benefits of smoking.

Crazy!

But that's what is happening as doctors who either run or work for gender clinics are being cited as experts. Anyone who does not support the transgender ideology is dismissed with ad hominem attacks as a hateful transphobe.

When talking to your children about authority, do it carefully. It is important for children to have a healthy respect for authority figures. One of the dangers of the transgender ideology is how it undermines authority figures in children's lives by telling them that their doctor misgendered them at birth, or that their parents were unable to tell that they were born in the wrong body, or than anyone who doesn't accept the transgender ideology is a hateful bigot.

Encourage children to think about the authority figures in their lives, and what the expertise is of those authority figures. For example, children would know that if they need a cavity filled, they go to a dentist, not to their pastor or teacher.

Bandwagon Fallacy

Bandwagoning is using the argument that "Everyone is doing it" or "All my friends get to" or "Everyone I know accepts this."

The idea is that if enough people believe something or think something or behave a certain way, then it must be okay. The response many of us older folks got when we were kids and tried to use a bandwagon fallacy to get what we wanted was, "If all your friends were jumping off a cliff, would you jump off too?" or something similarly sarcastic.

These days it seems that bandwagoning is the rule of the day, but we need to teach children that just because a lot of people believe something, it doesn't mean it is true. There are many examples throughout history where people got things wrong. Help your child understand that your family's values should guide their behavior, and how to avoid mindlessly following the crowd.

Bandwagoning works because most of us want to fit in, so children have to be taught that standing up to the crowd when it is wrong is far more important than going along with the crowd to fit in. Point out historical figures who stood up for what was right and changed the world by standing up for their values. Point out also where bandwagoning had horrifying outcomes, such as in Nazi Germany.

***

Rather than view teaching your children about logical fallacies as a chore, have fun with it! Make it a game for members of your family to spot them in advertisements or political debates, or even in day-to-day activities.

Logical fallacies are easy to use as examples because they don't require a lot of thought, but if you teach kids to think critically and understand the importance of upholding family values and having sound logical arguments, you will be providing them with skills that will help them throughout their lives.

There are many other logical fallacies in addition to those outlined here. One of the reasons transgender ideology has taken hold so strongly is that activists manipulate others with logical fallacies as they systematically indoctrinate those who are vulnerable and needy.

Arm your children with critical thinking skills and they will be able to spot the logical fallacies in the transgender ideology, even if they don't remember the specific type of fallacy being employed.

ENCOURAGING AN INTERNAL LOCUS OF CONTROL

The backbone of the transgender ideology is an external locus of control.

A locus of control can be internal or external.

Locus of control is a belief about how the world works. If children believe they have control over their thoughts and circumstances, they have an internal locus of control. If they believe that outside forces control them, they have an external locus of control. Children who have an internal locus of control tend to be less anxious and more successful because they believe they have control over themselves. Children who have an external locus of control are easily manipulated because they don't realize that they control their thoughts and feelings, as well as how they react to life's challenges.

Reinforcing an internal locus of control will help a child rebuff recruitment into the transgender ideology, which is based on an external locus of control. Do this by teaching children that they have the ability to change what they do to get different outcomes. If a child does well on a test, instead of saying, "You are smart," say "You worked hard," or "You paid attention in class." This will reinforce the idea that what they do has an impact on outcomes.

If a child is struggling with something, encourage her to believe she can change her circumstances. Give her examples of times in her life where she did something to change a situation.

Children who adopt a transgender identity are convinced that something in the world put them into the wrong body, and that others can harm them simply by using a different name than they would like, or not using the pronouns they prefer.

Children need to know that they have control over how they respond to their feelings.

For example, say a child is angry.

That child has a choice about how to respond to anger. The child can stomp his feet or he can hit someone, or he can cry, or he can tell someone how he is feeling. Anger is a signal that something is wrong, but it does not dictate a specific response. That is something the child gets to control.

BOUNDARIES

Parents can find themselves wanting to be friends with their children. This is understandable—our kids are amazing! But what children need are parents who set firm boundaries, rather than parents who are buddies.

There are lots of books about setting boundaries, so I will just briefly touch upon one of the most important boundaries today's parents need to create.

Every detransitioner I have interviewed has reported that social media had a significant impact on their adoption of a transgender identity.

There are predators on social media sites who set out to groom children into the transgender ideology. There is even a term for it: *cracking an egg*—the egg being a child.[162]

These groomers will ever so gently lead your child into the transgender ideology using all the tactics discussed previously.

Once a child believes he or she has been born in the wrong body, the groomer will provide a script the child can use to tell parents, as well as a script to tell health-care providers.[163]

There are even guidebooks specifically for children on how to tell others about having a transgender identity.[164]

Adolescent therapist Lisa Marchiano, in her article "Outbreak: On Transgender Teens and Psychic Epidemics," discusses how social media is fueling the transgender ideology, noting that "reports online indicate that a young person's coming out as transgender is often preceded by increased social media use and/or having one or more peers also come out as transgender. These factors suggest that social contagion may be contributing to the significant rise in the number of young people seeking treatment for gender dysphoria."[165]

James Caspian, who has worked extensively with those indoctrinated by the transgender ideology, says, "A lot of them will say they've spent a lot of time on social media where they've seen a lot of people have transitioned, feeling it was very cool..."[166]

Lisa Littman found a strong connection between social media use and tweens and teens adopting a transgender identity in her study on rapid-onset gender dysphoria.[167]

Additionally, the way in which social media is set up can induce something of a hypnotic trance as they scroll through posts.[168] Children in a trance can more easily be indoctrinated.

As they scroll through post after post, they are likely to see messages that promote the transgender ideology.

I strongly suggest having computers for children in public areas, not allowing children to have smartphones until they are at least 16, not allowing children to take phones or computers to their rooms at night, and limiting free time on computers to an hour or less a day. Also get good parental controls on your computer. Be aware that children are often more savvy with computers than parents. They will circumvent unsophisticated controls, so invest in a good system to protect your family.

Children will not be thrilled about the boundaries you set, and part of their development is to push against the boundaries to see how firm they are. When it comes to computer time and social media, your boundaries need to be solid.

HOUSEKEEPING

There is an important principle that parents need to remember.

When I was training to be an EMT, the first thing that they emphasize is that you can't help someone else if you're not in a position where you are safe.

If somebody is drowning, you do not jump in to save them because, more often than not, that person will drown you. You make sure you are well anchored, and then you throw the person in distress a life preserver.

If there's somebody lying in the street who's been shot, you have to make sure that you're safe from gunfire before you run out to help them. Otherwise you could get shot too.

This principle applies to protecting your children from the transgender ideology. If you are not functioning well, it is going to be more difficult for you to protect your family. It's important for parents to find ways of good self-care so that they have the energy and resources to focus on their children.

Parents almost always try to do right by their children; however, some parents struggle with anger, addiction, depression, marital strife, and other issues that interfere with their ability to parent. If you struggle with any difficulties that make it hard to parent, consider getting help.

You need to be the best parent you can be in order to protect your children from the transgender ideology.

CONCLUSION

"Political language is designed to make lies sound truthful and murder respectable

~ George Orwell[169]

With claims of being oppressed and marginalized, transgender activists have systematical captured society. Schools, media outlets, government officials, health-care practitioners, and businesses are all capitulating to transgender activist's demands, knowing that failing to do so will result in harassment and bullying.

For a kid who doesn't fit in, transgender activists provide support groups and clubs—all the child has to do is announce a transgender identity. That kid who didn't fit in now has friends, allies, and acceptance. The less the child conforms to social norms and claims to be victimized by others, the more support transgender activists provide.

Children are being converted to what is akin to a cultic religion with beliefs in supernatural powers that can place the gender spirit of one sex into the body of another.

Children are taught that it is sinful to use the wrong name or pronouns of someone who claims a transgender identity.

Each step along the pathway to modification of external appearance is a rite of passage, from social transitioning to puberty blockers to hormones to surgery.

The irony is, most of those who embrace transgender ideology don't even recognize it as a religion. They are so indoctrinated that they believe they have found the big "T" truth while professing that everyone has their own truth. Truth be told, they reject anyone who does not ascribe to their truth.

In addition to equipping your family with skills to resist indoctrination into the transgender ideology, there are some simple things you can do to help bring an end to this destructive movement.

Anytime there is a hearing or proposed policy on the local, state, or federal level, make a submission to the committee charged with deciding the policy. Something as simple as, "I disagree with this policy" is helpful—if you can give some specific reasons why you disagree, it is even more helpful. It is critical that we fight against policies that require children to lie and undermine important sex-based rights and protections.

Contact companies that are promoting transgender ideology. Let them know that you disagree and will not support them.

Subscribe to organizations that have action alerts and updates.

Engage in a letter-writing campaign to your legislators.

Request books that challenge the transgender ideology for your local libraries and school libraries.

Share your concerns with faith leaders and other community leaders.

Share Advocate Protecting Children memes on your social media accounts: https://www.advocatesprotectingchildren.org/meme-series.

These are just a few simple things everyone can do, and if enough people voice their concerns about the dangers of accepting the transgender ideology, things will start to change...making this book and others like it obsolete.

RESOURCES

Advocates Protecting Children
advocatesprotectingchildren.org

Child & Parental Rights Campaign
Navigating the Transgender Landscape-School Resource Guide
https://childparentrights.org/school-resource-guide

Generally Accepted Professional Medical Standards Determination on the Treatment of Gender Dysphoria (Florida)
https://www.ahca.myflorida.com/letkidsbekids/docs/AHCA_GAPM S_June_2022_Report.pdf

Minnesota Family Council
Parent Resource Guide
https://www.mfc.org/request-the-parent-resource-guide

Parents of ROGD Kids Support Group
https://www.parentsofrogdkids.com

Society for Evidence-Based Gender Medicine
https://www.segm.org

Transgender Trend
https://www.transgendertrend.com

Truth Is The New Hate Speech
https://www.youtube.com/c/ErinBrewer/videos

Understanding Transgender Issues
https://www.familywatch.org/transgenderissues

WoLF Media Style Guide
https://www.womensliberationfront.org/news/wolf-media-style-guide

OTHER BOOKS BY
ADVOCATES PROTECTING CHILDREN

Desist, Detrans, & Detox: Getting Your Child Out of the Gender Cult: A book for parents on why gender ideology is harmful and untrue, and how parents can extricate their children from the ideology.

Transing Our Children: A primer on the transgender industry and transgender ideology.

Always Erin: An autobiographical children's book about sexual assault, gender dysphoria, and how appropriate mental health care can bring a child back to health and safety.

Commonsense Care: The edited transcripts from the Commonsense Care Video Series.

ABOUT THE AUTHOR

Erin Brewer grew up in Salt Lake City.

She went on to earn a BS from Hampshire College. After getting her Master's and PhD from Utah State University, she was a stay-at-home mom and homeschool teacher for about ten years.

During this time, she also volunteered at a number of local agencies and ran her own produce business.

She is co-founder of the Compassion Coalition, an international group for those fighting to ban invasive, harmful, unproven medical interventions for gender-confused children; as well as Advocates Protecting Children an organization, that raises awareness and supports efforts to stop the unethical treatment of children by schools, hospitals, and mental and medical health-care providers under the duplicitous banner of *gender identity affirmation*.

GLOSSARY

Ally: a person who supports all LGB/TQ issues and ideologies. This is becoming more and more subjective, as many transgender-rights activists argue that homosexuals are transphobic if they refuse to date transgender-identified people who claim to be their preferred sex partners.

Androgynous: of indeterminate sex; having characteristics of both maleness and femaleness.

Antagonists: as used in this book, people who are leading your child deeper into the gender cult.

Asexual: not experiencing sexual attraction to others.

Biological Sex: the sex that one was born in—male or female—as evidenced by chromosomes, external anatomy (genitals, breasts), and internal anatomy (sex glands and organs) and most importantly, the type of gametes the individual does or did or will or would, produce but for developmental or genetic anomalies.

Biphobia: prejudice against bisexual people. In the current vernacular, this term is applied to anyone who disagrees with anything that a bisexual person says, wants, or believes.

Bisexual: experiencing sexual attraction to both males and females.

Desister: a person who believed him- or herself to be transgender, but has since accepted his or her birth sex as reality.

Detransitioner: a person who presented as other than his or her birth sex, transitioning socially and/or medically, but has since accepted his or her birth sex as reality and presents as such.

FTM: female to male transgender. Opposite of **MTF**.

Gender Clinic: a center that engages in experimental medical interventions, where nearly every child is encouraged to change their appearance both socially and medically.

Gender Dysphoria: a diagnostic term describing when one's sense of his/her gender identity does not always and/or fully match his/her biological sex.

Gender-Expansive: a term related to the ideology that gender is on a spectrum, and that one can be located anywhere on that spectrum.

Gender Expression: one's external presentation of one's gender identity; dressing and behaving like a particular sex or combination of the sexes, based upon stereotypes.

Gender Fluid: not ascribing to one fixed gender; one whose sense of gender identity changes frequently or all the time.

Gender Identity: a nonsensical term referring to one's self-perception as male, female, or something in between; based entirely on stereotypes.

Gender-Nonconforming: not aligning with stereotypes of one's biological sex.

Genderqueer: someone who embraces gender fluidity, who doesn't present according to biological sex stereotypes. Near synonym to **Nonbinary**.

Gender Transition: attempting to change sexes (or gender expression) or to impersonate another sex (or gender expression) via social transitioning (dressing according to stereotypes of a different sex) or medical transition (taking puberty blockers and/or cross-sex hormones, and/or having surgeries). Gender transitioning is an attempt to make the body align with the mind.

Glitter Families: transgender-identified adults who groom children to reject their families of origin and consider the transgender-identified adults their new families.

GLSEN (Gay, Lesbian & Straight Education Network): an organization that creates and disseminates homosexual and transgender propaganda, policy, and curricula.

Grooming: specific strategies used by child predators to gain access to children for their sexual exploitation.

HRC (the Human Rights Campaign Foundation): the funding and lobby organization for the homosexual and transgender communities.

Intersex: in popular, current usage, a person who was born with mixed anatomical features of maleness and femaleness. In one recent study, the sex of a newborn was not clear from inspection of genitalia in about 1 in 1,000 births. These individual have *disorders of sexual development*. Chromosomes and internal organs can be evaluated to clarify a child's sex. Some disorders of sexual development might not be discovered until puberty, or after.

MTF: male to female transgender. Opposite of **FTM.**

Nonbinary: someone who does not view himself or herself as aligning with either maleness or femaleness.

Pansexual: sexually attracted to anyone at anytime; willing to be sexual partners with anyone.

Peak (verb): recognizing that gender ideology is unsound; becoming gender-critical.

Presentation [or Present (verb)]: how one shows him or herself to the world; the clothing, hairstyle, and mannerism choices that reflect one's gender (sex) status, based on cultural stereotypes.

Queer: an umbrella term to express any sexual and/or gender orientation/presentation other than being a **cis-gender** heterosexual. Near antonym to **Cis-gender**.

Questioning: describes someone who is exploring his or her sexuality and/or gender.

Sex Assigned at Birth: one's biological sex. This term has been created to propagate the false idea that there is no such thing as biological sex, only the gender that someone (a doctor or parent) "assigned" to a child based on the child's genitalia.

Sexual Orientation: the nature of one's sexual and/or romantic attractions. LGB/TQ organizations often claim that sexual orientation is inherent and immutable, but this assertion is belied by the number of people who "come out" as homosexual in middle age or beyond, and those who became or returned to being heterosexual after counseling and/or therapy.

Stereotype: a widely-held idea or image of a person that is fixed and oversimplified (e.g., "all girls like pink," "all boys like sports," "women can't do math," etc.).

Supportive: willing to capitulate to all demands of the transgender-identified person.

Unsupportive: unwilling to capitulate to all demands of the transgender-identified person.

ENDNOTES

[1] Orwell, George, 1944. "The Freedom of the Press." *Times Literary Supplement*, September 15, 1972.

[2] Orwell, George. "Shooting an Elephant." *Politics and the English Language.* Penguin Classics, 1950.

[3] *Family Life and HIV Education for Junior Secondary Schools Student's Handbook*, 2nd ed. Action Health Incorporated, 2014.

[4] *Comprehensive Sexuality Education (CSE) Manual for Out of School Youth.* Department of Youth, Malawi, 2017.

[5] Orwell, George. *Politics and the English Language.* Penguin Classics, 1950.

[6] "Trans Umbrella Resource Sheet" ILACADA 2014-1. https://www.nacada.ksu.edu/Portals/0/CandIGDivision/documents/Trans%20 Umbrella%20Resource%20Sheet%20ILACADA%202014-1.pdf Accessed June 29, 2022.

[7] "Master List of Genders." Nonbinary School of Survival. https://nonbinary-school-survival.tumblr.com/post/125681867336/masterlist-of-genders Accessed July 19, 2022.

[8] "People are identifying as cake gender." Libs of TikTok. https://twitter.com/libsoftiktok/status/1524492898774884353?ref_src=twsrc %5Etfw%7Ctwcamp%5Etweetembed%7Ctwterm%5E152449289877488435 3%7Ctwgr%5E%7Ctwcon%5Es1_&ref_url=https%3A%2F%2Fwww.thebla ze.com%2Fnews%2Fcake-gender-libs-of-tiktok. "Stop the madness: Libs of TikTok posts video of a person discussing 'cake gender.'" Blaze Media, 2022. https://www.theblaze.com/news/cake-gender-libs-of-tiktok.

[9] "Sexual Orientation and Gender Identity Definitions." Human Rights Campaign. https://www.hrc.org/resources/sexual-orientation-and-gender-identity-terminology-and-definitions?utm_source=GS&utm_medium=AD&utm_campaign=BPI-HRC-Grant&utm_content=454887071989&utm_term=gender%20identity&gclid= CjwKCAjwx46TBhBhEiwArA_DjFMaaFRDD4j9saVhWYPKQquyAX6gct qSrojQlJ56ALhWEUeZuHYPIBoCRiwQAvD_BwE Accessed July 29, 2022.

[10] Lambert, Michael. "NYC Human Rights Commission Adds 31 Genders to Civil Rights Protections." Out.com, May 30, 2016. https://www.out.com/news-opinion/2016/5/30/nyc-human-rights-commission-adds-31-genders-civil-rights-protections.

[11] "Facebook launches 50 new gender options for users." PBS News Hour, February 13, 2014. https://www.pbs.org/newshour/nation/facebook-launches-50-new-gender-options-users#:~:text=The%20new%20options%20%E2%80%94%20which%20include,option%20of%20sharing%20the%20gender.

[12] LGBTQ Center OC—Zoom Schedule. LGBTQ Center OC. https://docs.google.com/spreadsheets/d/1se7y1-o8qBRiZ2klNm3JEpBBPpcfRVVOnWnDYdG3zQ4/edit#gid=0 Accessed July 19, 2022.

[13] "Changing Sex on Birth Certificates." House Bill 509, Idaho Vital Statistics Act. https://youtu.be/096_5Hc6PGc Accessed July 19, 2022.

[14] "Changing Birth Certificate Sex Designations: State-By-State Guidelines." Lambda Legal. https://www.lambdalegal.org/know-your-rights/article/trans-changing-birth-certificate-sex-designations Accessed June 29, 2022.

[15] Joyce, Helen. *Trans: When Ideology Meets Reality*. Oneword Publications, 2021.

[16] "Can Having Genital Preferences for Dating Mean You're Anti-Trans?" https://everydayfeminism.com/2017/04/cissexist-say-never-date-trans/ Accessed June 29, 2022.

[17] "Middle schoolers accused of sexual harassment for not using preferred pronouns, parents say." https://www.kktv.com/2022/05/16/middle-schoolers-accused-sexual-harassment-not-using-preferred-pronouns-parents-say/ Accessed June 29, 2022.

[18] "Professor disciplined for refusing to use transgender student's pronouns to receive $400K in settlement." https://thehill.com/changing-america/respect/diversity-inclusion/3273029-professor-disciplined-for-refusing-to-use-transgender-students-pronouns-to-receive-400k-in-settlement/ Accessed June 29, 2022.

[19] Brown, Lee. "Transgender kids OK for hormones at 14, surgery at 15, health group says" *New York Post*. https://nypost.com/2022/06/16/trans-kids-ok-for-hormones-at-14-surgery-at-15-health-group/?utm_source=NYPTwitter&utm_campaign=SocialFlow&utm_medium=SocialFlow.

[20] Id.

[21] Wong, Wallace. February 27, 2019. https://vimeo.com/326339802.

[22] "Top 10 Tips for Reporting on Suicide." American Foundation for Suicide Research. https://chapterland.org/wp-content/uploads/sites/13/2018/06/13763_TopTenNotes_Reporting_on_Suicide_Flyer_m1.pdf.

[23] "Vulnerable Child Protection Legislation." Texas Hearings Senate Bills 1311 and 64. https://youtu.be/RxAtDk5wXh4.

[24] Dr. Kevin Stuart's Testimony on SB 131. https://youtu.be/zhRW02Sn3Nw.

[25] Greene, Jay. "Puberty Blockers, Cross-Sex Hormones, and Youth Suicide." https://www.heritage.org/gender/report/puberty-blockers-cross-sex-hormones-and-youth-suicide Accessed July 19, 2022.

[26] "FDA: Don't Leave Childhood Depression Untreated." https://archive.org/details/ucm-413390 Accessed July 19, 2022.

[27] Iannelli, Vincent. "Off-Label Prescribing in Pediatrics." June 26, 2022. https://www.verywellhealth.com/prozac-for-kids-2632404

[28] "Understanding Transgender Issues: An Interview with Dr. Patrick Lappert." https://vimeo.com/498679928 Accessed July 19, 2022.

[29] Zucker, K. J. "Different strokes for different folks." *Child and Adolescent Mental Health Journal*, 2016.

[30] *Growing up Trans*, Season 2015, Episode 11. PBS. https://www.pbs.org/video/frontline-growing-up-trans/.

[31] "Understanding Transgender Issues: Interview with Dr. Michelle Cretella." https://vimeo.com/498975226 Accessed July 19, 2022.

[32] Ryan, Caitlin, Russell B. Toomey, Rafael M. Diaz & Stephen T. Russell. "Parent-Initiated Sexual Orientation Change Efforts With LGBT Adolescents: Implications for Young Adult Mental Health and Adjustment." *Journal of Homosexuality.* 2020: 67:2, 159–173. DOI: 10.1080/00918369.2018.1538407.

[33] "The Hidden Dangers Of Cosmetic Surgery." June 16, 2011. https://www.forbes.com/sites/jennagoudreau/2011/06/16/hidden-dangers-of-cosmetic-surgery/?sh=e60a1857b2bc Accessed July 19, 2022.

[34] Dhejne, Cecilia, et al. "Long-Term Follow-Up of Transsexual Persons Undergoing Sex Reassignment Surgery: Cohort Study in Sweden." *PLOS One.* 2011:6 e16885 (figures omitted).

[35] Lavrakas, P. J. *Encyclopedia of survey research methods* (Vols. 1–0). Thousand Oaks, CA: Sage Publications, Inc., 2008. DOI: 10.4135/9781412963947.

[36] Starr, Susan. "Survey research: we can do better." *Journal of the Medical Library Association*: JMLA vol. 100, 1 (2012): 1–2. DOI: 10.3163/1536-5050.100.1.001.

[37] Loftus, Elizabeth F. & Katherine Ketcham. *The Myth of Repressed Memory: False Memories and Allegations of Sexual Abuse*. New York: St. Martin's Press, 1994. Print.

[38] Tayeh A. & S. Cairncross. "The reliability of retrospective studies using a one-year recall period to measure dracunculiasis prevalence in Ghana." *Int J Epidemiol.* December 24, 1995: 24(6):1233–9. DOI: 10.1093/ije/24.6.1233. PMID: 8824868.

[39] van der Sluis, W.B., M.B. Bouman, N.K. de Boer, M.E. Buncamper, A.A. van Bodegraven, E.A. Neefjes-Borst, B.P. Kreukels, W.J. Meijerink, & M.G. Mullender. "Long-Term Follow-Up of Transgender Women After Secondary Intestinal Vaginoplasty." *J Sex Med.* April 13, 2016: 13(4):702–10. DOI: 10.1016/j.jsxm.2016.01.008. Epub, February 24, 2016. PMID: 26928775.

[40] Asscheman H., E.J. Giltay, J.A. Megens, W.P. de Ronde, M.A. van Trotsenburg, & L.J. Gooren. "A long-term follow-up study of mortality in transsexuals receiving treatment with cross-sex hormones." *Eur J Endocrinol.* April 2011: 164(4):635–42. DOI: 10.1530/EJE-10-1038. Epub, January 25, 2011. PMID: 21266549.

[41] Leriche, Albert, Marc-Olivier Timsit, Nicolas Morel-Journel, André Bouillot, Diala Dembele, & Alain Ruffion. "Long-term outcome of forearm free-flap phalloplasty in the treatment of transsexualism." First published January 08, 2008. https://DOI.org/10.1111/j.1464-410X.2007.07362.x.

[42] Kuiper, B. & P. Cohen-Kettenis. "Sex reassignment surgery: a study of 141 Dutch transsexuals." *Arch Sex Behav.* October 17, 1988: (5):439–57. DOI: 10.1007/BF01542484. PMID: 3219066.

[43] "Saving Women's Lives: Strategies for Improving Breast Cancer Detection and Diagnosis." J.E. Joy, E.E. Penhoet & D.B. Petitti, eds. *Institute of Medicine (US) and National Research Council (US) Committee on New Approaches to Early Detection and Diagnosis of Breast Cancer,* Appendix D, "Common Weaknesses in Study Designs." Washington DC: National Academies Press (US), 2005. Available from: https://www.ncbi.nlm.nih.gov/books/NBK22323/.

[44] Brewer, Erin & Maria Keffler. *Transing Our Children*. Partners for Ethical Care, 2021.

[45] Dettori, Joseph R. "Loss to follow-up." *Evidence-Based Spine-Care Journal*: vol. 2, 1:7–10 (2011). DOI: 10.1055/s-0030-1267080.

[46] Rehman J., S. Lazer, A.E. Benet, L.C. Schaefer & A. Melman. "The reported sex and surgery satisfactions of 28 postoperative male-to-female transsexual patients." *Arch Sex Behav.* February 28, 1999(1): 71–89. DOI: 10.1023/a:1018745706354. PMID: 10097806.

[47] Ruppin U. & F. Pfäfflin. "Long-Term Follow-Up of Adults with Gender Identity Disorder." *Arch Sex Behav.* July 2015: 44(5):1321–9. DOI: 10.1007/s10508-014-0453-5. Epub, February 18 2015. PMID: 25690443.

[48] Veronica Pimenoff & Friedemann Pfäfflin. "Transsexualism: Treatment Outcome of Compliant and Noncompliant Patients." *International Journal of Transgenderism* 2011: 13:1, 37–44. DOI: 10.1080/15532739.2011.618399.

[49] van der Sluis, W.B. "Long-Term Follow-Up of Transgender Women After Secondary Intestinal Vaginoplasty." DOI: 10.1016/j.jsxm.2016.01.008. PMID: 26928775.

[50] Lindqvist, E.K., H. Sigurjonsson, C. Möllermark, et al. "Quality of life improves early after gender reassignment surgery in transgender women." *Eur J Plast Surg,* 2017: 40, 223–226. https://doi.org/10.1007/s00238-016-1252-0.

[51] Bränström, Richard Pachankis, John. "Reduction in Mental Health Treatment Utilization Among Transgender Individuals After Gender-Affirming Surgeries: A Total Population Study." *American Journal of Psychiatry,* October 4, 2019 https://doi.org/10.1176/appi.ajp.2019.19010080

[52] Van Mol, Andre, Michael Kaidlaw, Miriam Grossman, & Paul McHugh. September 13, 2020 Correction: "Transgender Surgery Provides No Mental Health Benefit." https://www.thepublicdiscourse.com/2020/09/71296/ Accessed July 19, 2022.

[53] Dhejne, Cecilia, et al. "Long-Term Follow-Up of Transsexual Persons Undergoing Sex Reassignment Surgery: Cohort Study in Sweden." *PLOS One.* 2011: 6:e16885 (figures omitted).

[54] O'Bodlund, Kullgren G. "Transsexualism—general outcome and prognostic factors: a five-year follow-up study of nineteen transsexuals in the process of changing sex." *Arch Sex Behav.* June 25, 1996: 25(3):303–16. DOI: 10.1007/BF02438167. PMID: 8726553.

[55] van der Sluis, W.B. "Long-Term Follow-Up of Transgender Women After Secondary Intestinal Vaginoplasty." DOI: 10.1016/j.jsxm.2016.01.008. PMID: 26928775.

[56] Sørensen, T.A. "Follow-up study of operated transsexual females." *Acta Psychiatr Scand.* July 1981: 64(1):50–64. DOI: 10.1111/j.1600-0447.1981.tb00760.x. PMID: 7315494.

[57] Turban, J.L., D. King, J. Kobe, S.L. Reisner & A.S. Keuroghlian. "Access to gender-affirming hormones during adolescence and mental health outcomes among transgender adults." *PLOS One.* 2017(1): e0261039. https://doi.org/10.1371/journal.pone.0261039.

[58] Levine, Dr. Rachel. Twitter, January 24, 2020. https://twitter.com/secretarylevine/status/1220745104605843457 Accessed July 19, 2022.

[59] Biggs, Michael. "Puberty Blockers and Suicidality in Adolescents Suffering from Gender Dysphoria." *Archives of Sexual Behavior,* June 3, 2020. https://link.springer.com/article/10.1007/s10508-020-01743-6.

[60] Id.

[61] Field, Scott S. & Den A. Trumbull. "RE: Pubertal Suppression for Transgender Youth and Risk of Suicidal Ideation" *Pediatrics,* February 2020. https://pediatrics.aappublications.org/content/145/2/e20191725/tab-e-letters#re-pubertal-suppression-for-transgender-youth-and-risk-of-suicidal-ideation.

[62] Id.

[63] Id.

[64] Biggs, Michael. "Puberty Blockers…" https://link.springer.com/article/10.1007/s10508-020-01743-6.

[65] Id.

[66] D'Angelo, Roberto, et al. "One Size Does Not Fit All: In Support of Psychotherapy for Gender Dysphoria." *Archives of Sexual Behavior,* 2021: 50:7–16. https://link.springer.com/article/10.1007/s10508-020-01844-2.

[67] "Trans Health & Medical Care: Where We Are, Where We Came From: An Obermann Conversation." https://youtu.be/j9ppfM1D6Qs

[68] Bailey, J. Michael & Ray Blanchard. "Suicide or transition: The only options for gender dysphoric kids?" *4th Wave Now,* September 8, 2017. https://4thwavenow.com/2017/09/08/suicide-or-transition-the-only-options-for-gender-dysphoric-kids/.

[69] Orwell, George. *Nineteen Eighty-Four.* Penguin Classics.

[70] Blanchard, Ray. Twitter: @BlanchardPhD, May 22, 2018. https://twitter.com/blanchardphd/status/998939098562916352

[71] "How to simulate a period (for transgender women)." Precious Stars Vlogs, September 2015. https://youtu.be/BcNco-mM700.

[72] Adams. "MtFtM Detransition 5—Q&A." https://youtu.be/0ULb3kG_21c.

[73] "Exclusive: NY Democrats Quietly Dismantle '1 Male, 1 Female' Rule." The Velvet Chronicle. https://thevelvetchronicle.com/ny-democrats-quietly-dismantle-1-male-1-female-rule/.

[74] Heggen, Ute. *In the Curated Woods*. iUniverse, 2022

[75] "Doctor Defends 'Gender Affirming' Interventions." https://youtu.be/L84QKfXxQ9Q.

[76] Narang, Akshay. "Loser Will Thomas changed his gender to become Lia Thomas and crushed all records." https://tfiglobalnews.com/2022/03/19/loser-will-thomas-changed-his-gender-to-become-lia-thomas-and-crushed-all-records/ Accessed June 16, 2022.

[77] Brownstone, M. "That's Not A Female Weightlifter, It's A Man, Baby!" Women Are Human. https://www.womenarehuman.com/thats-not-a-female-weightlifter-its-a-man-baby/ Accessed June 16, 2022.

[78] McHenry, Britt. "Transgender Athletes Who Compete Against Women Are Cheats." https://thefederalist.com/2019/02/27/transgender-athletes-compete-women-cheats/ Accessed June 16, 2022.

[79] Slatz, Anna. "Male Serial Killer Housed At Washington Women's Prison." https://4w.pub/male-serial-killer-housed-at-washington-womens-prison/ Accessed June 16, 2022.

[80] Ngo, Andy. "Sex offending suspect claims transgender harassment in Wi Spa case." https://nypost.com/2021/09/02/charges-filed-against-sex-offender-in-wi-spa-casecharges-filed-against-sex-offender-in-notorious-wi-spa-incident/ Accessed June 16, 2022.

[81] "How do you know if your dysphoria is actually internalized misogyny? And does that change anything? How do you deal with internalized misogyny?" https://www.reddit.com/r/AskFeminists/comments/iomeoh/how_do_you_know_if_your_dysphoria_is_actually/ Accessed June 16, 2022.

[82] "Transgender Victim: Sydney's Story." https://familywatch.org/transgenderissues/#.Yqvx4JPML6M Accessed June 16, 2022.

[83] "Transing Away The Gay: Kai." https://youtu.be/63ltTReosrk .

[84] "Masquerading As A Woman." https://www.youtube.com/watch?v=qbCX8XgvBMI&t=502s.

[85] "Transgender Victim: Bill's Story." https://familywatch.org/transgenderissues/#.Yqxtz5PML6M.

[86] Selmys, Melinda. "12 Causes of Gender Dysphoria." https://www.patheos.com/blogs/catholicauthenticity/2015/07/12-causes-of-gender-dysphoria/ Accessed June 17, 2022.

[87] "NHS child gender clinic: Staff welfare concerns 'shut down.'" BBC Newsnight. https://youtu.be/zTRnrp9pXHY.

[88] "Female detransition and reidentification: Survey results and interpretation." https://guideonragingstars.tumblr.com/post/149877706175/female-detransition-and-reidentification-survey

[89] "Testosterone, Mastectomy, Hysterectomy, Then Detransition, Ashira:" https://youtu.be/i0EFPv1_jdI.

[90] "Data & Statistics on Autism Spectrum Disorder." https://www.cdc.gov/ncbddd/autism/data.html.

[91] Kozlowska, Kasia, et al. "Human Systems: Therapy, Culture and Attachment, Australian children and adolescents with gender dysphoria: Clinical presentations and challenges experienced by a multidisciplinary team and gender service." https://journals.sagepub.com/DOI/full/10.1177/26344041211010777.

[92] "Female detransition and reidentification…" https://guideonragingstars.tumblr.com/post/149877706175/female-detransition-and-reidentification-survey

[93] "Sissy Porn and Silicon Valley." https://grahamlinehan.substack.com/p/sissy-porn-and-silicon-valley Accessed June 17, 2022.

[94] Personal communication with Petra Harangir. June 30, 2022.

[95] Littman, Lisa. "Parent reports of adolescents and young adults perceived to show signs of a rapid onset of gender dysphoria." https://journals.plos.org/plosone/article?id=10.1371/journal.pone.0202330.

[96] Shrier, Abigail. *Irreversible Damage.* Salem Media Group, 2020.

[97] "Vulnerable Child Protection Legislation." https://youtu.be/RxAtDk5wXh4.

[98] Personal communication with Petra Harangir. July 2022.

[99] Shrier, Abigail. "Inside Planned Parenthood's Gender Factory." https://abigailshrier.substack.com/p/inside-planned-parenthoods-gender Accessed June 17, 2022.

[100] Littman, Lisa. "Parent reports of adolescents…" https://journals.plos.org/plosone/article?id=10.1371/journal.pone.0202330

[101] TullipR/Richie. Twitter: @TullipR, June 13, 2022. https://twitter.com/TullipR/status/1536422533230206976 Accessed June 17, 2022.

[102] "Transing The Gay Away." https://youtu.be/JxQHnxHC2bE.

[103] Wright, Sydney. "Trans-Identity Development: Potential Causes." https://vimeo.com/manage/videos/490953579.

[104] Women's Voices, June 28, 2022 Twitter, https://twitter.com/WomenReadWomen/status/1541840380982956032?ref_src=twsrc%5Etfw.

[105] Shrier, Abigail. *Irreversible Damage*. Salem Media Group, 2020.

[106] Orwell, George. *Nineteen Eighty-Four*.

[107] "Poisoning Children: Planned Parenthood's New Business Plan." Partners for Ethical Care. https://youtu.be/Vr8rz8THpk0

[108] Van Mol, Andre. "Transgender Surgery Provides No Mental Health Benefit." https://www.youtube.com/watch?v=f4cX1ZdE8PY&t=802s

[109] Lappert, Dr. Patrick. "Veteran Plastic Surgeon: No One Is Born In The Wrong Body." https://youtu.be/wtG7rJdxAZg

[110] Van Meter, Dr. Quentin. "Pediatric Endocrinologist Fights Against Harmful Trans Ideology." https://youtu.be/lcYrDrzV7DY

[111] Levine, Dr. Stephen. "Pennsylvania Public Hearing on Appropriate Care Models for Transgender Adolescents." http://www.pahousegop.com/embed/24641/Public-hearing-on-Appropriate-Care-Models-for-Transgender-Adolescents-

[112] Hruz, Paul, Lawrence Mayer & Paul McHugh. "Growing Pains: Problems with Puberty Suppression in Treating Gender Dysphoria." The New Atlantis. https://www.thenewatlantis.com/publications/growing-pains.

[113] "Looking at suppressing puberty for transgender kids." Associated Press, March 12, 2016.

[114] "Transgender Youth Using Puberty Blockers." KQED, August 19, 2016.

[115] Alegría, Christine Aramburu. "Gender nonconforming and transgender children/youth: Family, community, and implications for practice." *Journal of the American Association of Nurse Practitioners,* October 1, 2016: 28 (10): 521–527. DOI:10.1002/2327-6924.12363. ISSN 2327-6924. PMID 27031444.

[116] "Current treatments for endometriosis." Mayo Clinic. https://www.mayoclinic.org/diseases-conditions/endometriosis/diagnosis-treatment/drc-20354661.

[117] Spears, Darcy. "More women come forward with complaints about Lupron side effects." February 12, 2019. https://www.ktnv.com/news/investigations/more-women-come-forward-with-complaints-about-lupron-side-effects Accessed July 19, 2022.

[118] Emmons, Libby. "Mom celebrates her teen's puberty-blocker induced early menopause. A mom took to the internet to croon with pride for her 15-year-old child who is undergoing early, medically induced, menopause." Brooklyn, NY, April 19, 2020.

[119] Klink D., M. Caris, A. Heijboer, M. van Trotsenburg & J. Rotteveel. "Bone Mass in Young Adulthood Following Gonadotropin-Releasing Hormone Analog Treatment and Cross-Sex Hormone Treatment in Adolescents With Gender Dysphoria." *J. Clinical Endo. & Met Ab.*, February 1, 2015: Vol. I 00(2) E270–E275. https://DOI.org/ I 0.121O/jc.2014-2439

[120] Biggs, Michael. "Tavistock's Experiment with Puberty Blockers." Department of Sociology, St Cross College, & University of Oxford. (version 1.0.1, July 29, 2019). http://users.ox.ac.uk/~sfos0060/Biggs_ExperimentPubertyBlockers.pdf

[121] Spears, Darcy. "Women fear drug they used to halt puberty led to health problems." PBS News Hour, February 4, 2017. https://www.pbs.org/newshour/health/women-fear-drug-they-used-to-halt-puberty-led-to-health-problems.

[122] "Lupron Victim Advocate Issues Urgent Warning." November 11, 2019. https://www.kelseycoalition.org/pubs/Lupron-Victim-Advocate-Issues-Urgent-Warning.

[123] Olson-Kennedy, Johanna. "The Impact of Early Medical Treatments in Transgender Youth." https://docs.wixstatic.com/ugd/3f4f51_a929d049f7fb46c7a72c4c86ba43869a.pdf.

[124] "The Hormone Health Crisis | with Endocrinologist William Malone, MD." https://youtu.be/z4RYl75zdMY.

[125] Orwell, George. *Nineteen Eighty-Four.*

[126] Curtis, J.M. "Factors related to susceptibility and recruitment by cults." *Psychol Rep.*, October 1993: 73(2):451–60. DOI: 10.2466/pr0.1993.73.2.451. PMID: 8234595.

[127] "Horrified Mother Gets Front Row Seat to Sex & Gender Indoctrination Strategy Meeting." https://www.partnersforethicalcare.com/post/horrified-mother-gets-front-row-seat-to-sex-gender-indoctrination-strategy-meeting Accessed June 19, 2022.

[128] "Testimony of Ronald N. Loomis in support of House Joint Resolution." May 25, 1999. https://web.archive.org/web/20040818214228/http:/religiousmovements.lib.virginia.edu/cultsect/mdtaskforce/loomis_testimony.htm Accessed June 19, 2022.

[129] "Transjacked: Former Trans Kid: Petra." https://youtu.be/DtXLQd05RQ4.

[130] "Cult Mind Control Techniques." https://sites.google.com/site/cultmindcontroltechniques/isolation Accessed June 19, 2022.

[131] "MtoF tells trans kids to dump moms on Mother's Day and join the 'glitter-queer' family of adult trans activists." https://4thwavenow.com/2017/05/14/mtof-tells-trans-kids-to-dump-moms-on-mothers-day-and-join-the-glitter-queer-family-of-adult-trans-activists/ Accessed June 19, 2022.

[132] Burton, H. *The Malleability of Memory: A Conversation with Elizabeth Loftus.* United Kingdom: Open Agenda Publishing, 2020.

[133] Walsh, Matt. "Matt Walsh Revisits His What Is A Woman Interview With Dr. Forcier." https://youtu.be/zdDB8wU73NA.

[134] "TRA violent threats Jul 5, 2018–Sep 3, 2021." https://photos.app.goo.gl/z2cbyxLSMsGEjEyKA.

[135] "10 Things to Know About the Psychology of Cults." https://www.onlinepsychologydegree.info/what-to-know-about-the-psychology-of-cults/ Accessed June 19, 2022.

[136] Curtis, J.M. "Factors related to…" DOI: 10.2466/pr0.1993.73.2.451. PMID: 8234595.

[137] "Mind Control." Freedom of Mind Resource Center. https://freedomofmind.com/cult-mind-control/bite-model/ Accessed June 19, 2022

[138] Herthel, J., J. Jennings, & S. McNicholas. *I am Jazz!* Dial Books for Young Readers, 2014.

[139] "Real Impact, Dr. Michael Laidlaw – 'Medical Harms from the Treatment of Child and Adolescent Gender Dysphoria.'" https://youtu.be/2iJHf1BKPJY.

[140] Truong, Debbie. *Longview News-Journal*, March 4, 2019. https://www.news-journal.com/virginia-school-spotlights-transgender-kids-in-event-supported-by-teachers-rights-group/article_2db916d4-3ec3-11e9-9bf1-c7b77f37c659.html.

[141] "HRC's Welcoming Schools." https://welcomingschools.org/ Accessed June 16, 2022.

[142] "Fairfax GOP Chairman Tim Hannigan Decries Transgender Ideology in Kindergarten." WMAL Newstalk 105.9, posted on March 5, 2019. https://www.wmal.com/2019/03/05/listen-fairfax-gop-chairman-tim-hannigan-decries-transgender-ideology-in-kindergarten/

[143] "Respect Responsibility." Advocates for Youth Rights. https://www.3rs.org/ Accessed June 16, 2022.

[144] Ibid.

[145] "The School Counselor and Transgender and Nonbinary Youth," Adopted 2016, revised 2022. American School Counselor Association. Accessed July 22, 2022.

[146] "Loudoun County 'Transgender' School Rapist Found Guilty.'" https://theparadise.ng/loudoun-county-transgender-school-rapist-found-guilty/ Accessed June 16, 2022.

[147] Swarts, Tracy. "CPS says new 'boys+' and 'girls+' bathroom signs are gender inclusive; petition seeks to rescind policy." December 14, 2021. https://www.chicagotribune.com/news/breaking/ct-chicago-public-schools-bathroom-policy-gender-20211214-shb3sqqgt5gxdbukqyxnypulem-story.html Accessed June 16, 2022.

[148] "Gender neutral toilets in schools aren't working." Transgender Trend. https://www.transgendertrend.com/gender-neutral-toilets-schools/ Accessed July 19, 2022.

[149] *Participant's Workbook*. UNFPA Comprehensive Sexuality Education for Out of School Young People in East and Southern Africa, 2017. https://drive.google.com/file/d/14zhlp0WfSrwg9Vl-xJaKyko-8pZcuRhr/view?usp=sharing.

[150] Orwell, George. *Nineteen Eighty-Four*.

[151] "Woman who sexually assaulted 10-year-old girl as teen will serve sentence in juvenile facility." https://abc7.com/hannah-tubbs-sexual-assault-california-child-molester-juvenile-facility/11516315/ Accessed June 17, 2022.

152 Kanter, Jake. "BBC 'altered gender in trans rape claim'." https://www.thetimes.co.uk/article/bbc-altered-gender-in-trans-rape-claim-3cqj73tq5 Accessed June 17, 2022.

153 Evon, Dan. "Did Blue's Clues Pride Parade Feature a Beaver with 'Top Scars'?" https://www.snopes.com/fact-check/blues-clues-pride-beaver-top-scars/ Accessed June 17, 2022.

154 Orwell, George. *Nineteen Eighty-Four.*

155 Orwell, George. *England, your England: And other essays.* London: Secker & Warburg, 1953.

156 "CSE Course for Teachers." UNESCO. https://csetraining.pathwright.com/library/cse-course-for-teachers-179303/402985/path/step/168522188/ Accessed June 20, 2022.

157 Lefory, Emily & Snejana Farberov. "Who is Xavier Musk, Elon's trans child who wants to change name to Vivian?" https://nypost.com/2022/06/21/who-is-xavier-musk-elon-musks-transgender-child-who-wants-to-change-name/?fbclid=IwAR0Km5e6nRh7GIyYlyv8WqyYiGMbrzRZiE9ZgZAU8GxzQAW9-rXovd2Qpd8 Accessed June 21, 2022.

158 "WoLF Releases New Media Style Guide For Journalists Reporting On Sex And Gender." https://www.womensliberationfront.org/news/wolf-media-style-guide Accessed June 21, 2022.

159 "US Transgender Survey." https://transequality.org/issues/us-trans-survey Accessed June 20, 2022.

160 Personal communication. July 3, 2022.

161 Garofalo, Dr. Robert. "Understanding Gender Nonconformity in Children and Adolescents." https://youtu.be/zcJYq9U3v74.

162 "Egg." https://www.urbandictionary.com/define.php?term=Egg Accessed June 29, 2022.

163 "Coming Out Trans To Your Parents & Family." https://lgbtrc.usc.edu/files/2015/05/Coming-Out-as-Trans.pdf Accessed June 29, 2022.

164 "Coming Out." https://www.lgbtyouth.org.uk/media/1054/coming-out-guide-for-t-people.pdf Accessed June 29, 2022

165 Marchiano, Lisa. "Outbreak: On Transgender Teens and Psychic Epidemics." https://www.tandfonline.com/DOI/full/10.1080/00332925.2017.1350804

166 "Detransitioning: Reversing a gender transition." BBC Newsnight. https://youtu.be/fDi-jFVBLA8.

[167] Littman, Lisa. "Rapid-onset gender dysphoria in adolescents and young adults: A study of parental reports." *PLOS One*. 2018: 13. e0202330. 10.1371/journal.pone.0202330.

[168] Hassen, Steven. *Freedom of Mind.* Freedom of Mind Press, 2022.

[169] Orwell, G. "Shooting an Elephant."

Made in the USA
Coppell, TX
22 May 2023

17164687R00090